The ABC's of MAN ON PURPOSE

26 Steps to Become the Man You Are Intended to Be

RICHARD A. RICE

Copyright © 2015 Richard Rice

ISBN-10:0692574794
ISBN-13: 978-0692574799 (MAN ON PURPOSE)

Cover Illustration by Richard Rice

Interior Design and Layout by Richard Rice

Author's Photograph by Beth Goff

Edited by Justin C. Hart

Printed by CREATESPACE

ISBN-10:0692574794
ISBN-13: 978-0692574799 (MAN ON PURPOSE)

http://manonpurpose.org

Give feedback on the book at:

admin@manonpurpose.org

FACEBOOK: MAN ON PURPOSE

TWITTER: @amanonpurpose

TABLE OF CONTENTS

CHAPTER   PAGE

INTRODUCTION v

ACKNOWLEDGEMENTS ix

CHAPTER 1 – A - ASK 1

CHAPTER 2 – B - BELIEVE 14

CHAPTER 3 – C - CHOOSE 22

CHAPTER 4 – D - DO 35

CHAPTER 5 – E - ENDURE 46

CHAPTER 6 – F - FAITH... 56

CHAPTER 7 – G - GIVE.. 66

CHAPTER 8 – H - HUMBLE 73

CHAPTER 9 – I - INTENTIONAL 80

CHAPTER 10 – J - JOY... 88

CHAPTER 11 – K - KNOCK 94

CHAPTER 12 – L - LOVE.. 103

CHAPTER 13 – M - MATURE 118

CHAPTER 14 – N - NEW 128

CHAPTER 15 – O - OBEDIENCE................................. 141

CHAPTER 16 – P - PURPOSE 153

CHAPTER 17 – Q - QUIET 163

CHAPTER 18 – R - RECEIVE 172

CHAPTER 19 – S - SACRIFICE 183

CHAPTER 20 – T - TRUST 194

CHAPTER 21– U - USABLE 208

CHAPTER 22 – V - VISION 220

CHAPTER 23 – W - WISDOM 230

CHAPTER 24 – X - XCELLENCE 241

CHAPTER 25 – Y - YOU 252

CHAPTER 26 – Z - ZEAL 265

AUTHORS TESTIMONY 275

INTRODUCTION

Men, I am so glad that you have decided to embark on this journey. Yes, I call it a journey because these ABC's cannot be learned in a day, a week, or even in a month. It may just take a lifetime. There are two important things that will help you learn the ABC's of becoming the man that you are intended to be: 1) God 2) time.

When walking with God we have to be intentional to see and learn the things that He has placed strategically in His Word. By all means, I have not arrived, nor do I have all the answers. In this book, I am simply sharing with you what I have learned throughout the years and what God has impressed upon me to put down on paper. Nothing comes magically to create change in us, however by applying these ABC's as a daily challenge, I believe it will help you to increase your relationship with God and become the man on purpose that He has called you to become.

Before 2015, I had been struggling for several years with the direction of my life. I knew that I was supposed to start this ministry called MAN ON PURPOSE - Becoming the man you are intended to be with purpose, on purpose. I remember receiving this idea one Saturday morning back in April of 2012, and like anyone else when they get a grand idea, I felt like a kid in a candy store. I immediately submitted to God's guidance and prepared myself for this journey. If there was going to be any significant change, I had to become the passenger in this endeavor. Little did I know, God had been grooming me all along.

Once my eyes were opened to the previous ministries that I had been involved with, I realized that they were foundational prerequisites for MAN ON PURPOSE. The vision that God impressed on me was to take all that I had learned up to that point in my life and help other men, both young and old, to be more intentional when seeking out their specific God-given purpose, identity and direction.

My experiences in the homeless ministry would ultimately be what allowed me to show brotherly love and have true compassion. I needed to be able to listen. Not just listen with my ears, but with my heart. An impactful ministry called Celebrate Recovery taught me how to do that. I needed to take initiative towards learning God's Word and sharing it with others. And that's what I began to do.

God was making such an amazing transformation within me. Through practice, I learned how to be transparent and share hidden truths with other men who were struggling with their "issues". God revealed the amazing power of Jesus to me and now I am able to show others how His grace works in and through each and every one of us.

That same year, I had the marvelous opportunity to be a part of John Maxwell's leadership program and learn leadership principles the way God intended. In four short months, I was able to gather a group of guys and put together my first men's event by August 2012. It was such a privilege! I had no idea how I was going to pull it off. I tell you, there is nothing more powerful than watching God at work. He can do more in a minute than you and I can do in a lifetime! This event was completely God orchestrated; all I had to do was be faithful, obedient, and intentional.

I won't go into the details here, but you can read the full story at the end of the book. I believe the complete story of MAN ON PURPOSE is a powerful one, simply because I did not create the idea. I believe it was given to me. All I did was continually *ask* God to show me my purpose, and here I am.

To be 100% honest with you, there were several challenges, several failures, and several times I gave into temptations. I even quit MAN ON PURPOSE a couple of times. You might wonder, *how does someone quit something that God has given them?* Easy! You quit for the moment. You lose hope. You give up. Nevertheless, if it is really a God-thing and truly your purpose, it will not leave you alone. Once it is assigned to you, you're on the journey for the long haul, my friend.

Let me put it like this: it becomes you. It is your forever stamp similar to your identity in Christ (2 Corinthians 5:17). Although I tried to give up my calling and my purpose, I kept asking God for guidance. Every single time I did so, God would return me to the same ministry He gave me back in April of 2012 like a boomerang.

Nearly three years later, while completing a spiritual fast during the early part of 2015, God impressed upon my heart to begin writing. And so I did. For three full days in the month of February I focused 100% on what He wanted me to write. In the back of my mind I thought, *I have started this thing too many times.* But my prayer was for God to show me His will. Ever since those three days, my job has been to remain compliant and do what He tells me. How else am I ever going to receive what He has for me if I don't listen to what He says?

That right there is what our lives have to be about. I cannot emphasize this enough. You must stop what you are doing and step into Him. Let God give you the answers to what you are seeking. But first, let me ask this question, "What are you seeking?"

If there is a hole in your heart that are you trying to fill, recognize that you cannot fill it with something tangible. More swings with the golf club won't do it, neither will big, metal play toys with engines, or alcohol, drugs, sex, and money. Nothing in this world will satisfy.

The only One that can satisfy and fill that void that you are hoping to fill is always going to be God, the One who created you; Why? Because He created you! He knows everything about you. He knows the things that you have no clue about. Men, understand that you can live this life doing everything your own way, which seems right in your own eyes, but just know this: IT DOESN'T WORK! The Bible says it this way:

There is a way that appears to be right, but in the end it leads to death. (Proverbs 14:12)

As you finish reading each chapter, take the time to reflect and meditate after each prayer. The challenge is to take each topic and create your own journal or short list of what you can do. For example,

when you finish reading chapter one, what are a few things that you could jot down and ask God about? You may not receive answers right away, but be intentional about asking and seeking. You will get answers soon enough.

To get the most out of this book it calls for active participation. By participating you will learn to be more intentional in everything. Being intentional is the key to your walk with Christ as well as your overall success in life. I pray this book blesses you beyond your expectations and mine...

My prayer is this: Lord, as men all over the world read the ABC's of this book, may they be empowered by Your grace to incorporate each of these teachings into their daily lives as they seek Your face and ask You for their own purpose, identity and direction. I pray that these teachings will be impressed upon their hearts for the benefit of glorifying You. I thank You, Lord for this MAN ON PURPOSE Ministry and the opportunity to further Your kingdom here on earth and be a part of so many men's lives.

In Jesus' name, AMEN!

ACKNOWLEDGEMENTS

I give a *very* special thank you to God for saving me, forgiving me, and showing me the love of Christ. I know without Him leading me to White Columns Inn in 2002, I would not be here today.

I must give Carrie, my awesome wife, a special thank you as well. I am grateful for your unconditional love, support, and patience. You were then, and you continue to be an amazing gift from God, my angel. Only God could have ever matched us two together, showing us how to make our many differences work together to build an amazing bond in our marriage. I am so very blessed to have you as my wife and partner. Thank you Carrie Rice for making this book a reality.

I thank Victory World Church in Norcross, Georgia with Pastor Dennis Rouse and his wife Colleen for making my first church experience a great one. It was because of their teaching and leadership, in addition to their warm, loving, and inviting environment that made it possible for me to grow in Christ and get to this point in my life.

Lastly, to all of the men who played a part in my journey; whether it was for a short or a long time, every moment we spent together helped in writing this book. I truly thank you...

CHAPTER ①

ASK Ⓐ

"Ask and it will be given to you; seek and you will find; knock and the door will be opened to you." (Matthew 7:7)

So, here we are. This is definitely the "A" or the first thing we need to do in order to live the life that God has planned for us to live. Anything and everything we need comes from asking. All we have to do is ask, that is it.

The Bible says in James "If any of you lacks wisdom, you should **ask** God, who gives generously to all without finding fault, and it will be given to you" (v1:5). Matthew says, "**Ask** and it will be given to you; seek and you will find; knock and the door will be opened to you" (v7:7).

I *had* to start this book off with something that is hard for men to do which is asking for things. Before any of the other letters of becoming the man God has intended us to become can be completed, and before He can activate what He wants to do in us and through us, we first have to humble ourselves and simply ask. I say simply ask here as if that is a simple thing for many of us to do. I know it's not easy. God didn't say that it was supposed to be easy either. He just said to ask.

I don't know about you, but for me, asking for things was never an easy task. Growing up as a kid in my household, I remember having to ask for everything. I mean everything. My siblings and I couldn't take one thing out of the refrigerator or the cabinets without having to ask our parents first. We had to ask about the clothes we were going to wear, if we could go outside, if we could ride bikes, if we could play with so and so, even if we could get a glass of water! The asking list goes on and on. We had to ask for literally everything! Most of the time, I just did without because I was too afraid to ask. I was physically and verbally abused throughout my childhood, so of course I was afraid of my parents, especially my father. So, eventually I just stopped asking for things.

There were times when my siblings and I would get together and say that it was the other one's turn to ask. My stepsister frequently got stuck with asking, because she was told "No" the least. Not only was I too afraid to ask, but I honestly got tired of it. I eventually preferred not to ask for anything and just be without.

When I moved out and left home at age 17, I surely did not have to ask for anything anymore. Or so I thought... I got to a point where if I wanted something I would just take it, even if I had to steal it. If I wanted it, it was mine. Now, clearly I'm not saying how I thought was right, because I know that it was not smart. But how many men have thought the same way? If it's going to be, it's up to me.

It wasn't until later in life that I began learning about what it means to ask for something. It was hard for me because I became so independent. I took on the mindset that in my own strength I could find what I wanted and make it mine. You see, I always thought that having to ask for things made me weak. I saw the person whom I needed to ask as being the one who had power or control over me. They could tell me "Yes" or "No", but I didn't want to be controlled. I had been controlled long enough when I was growing up. I wanted to be my own man; needing no one. And I mean no one. When someone offered to help me I told them, "I got it." Do you see that pride? Oops, did I say the "P" word? That word is another discussion for a later time.

Do you see how becoming a man can be defective if we are not careful? What I mean is this: we have been taught through the generations to be independent and self-sufficient. As men, we are supposed to have the answers to everything. We are to be strong and take charge. "You can do it!" is what we hear. If a man would dare ask for help, then he is seen as weak. Because of the "P" word, we think asking makes us look stupid or something.

But I found the exact opposite to be true.

I found an excerpt from www.psychcentral.com by Linda Sapadin, PHD. She asks and answers the following question by stating, "How come men don't operate rationally when they don't know something?

It is because men prefer to learn by doing, not by being told what to do."

I agree. This is why boys generally do not do as well as girls do in school. They don't want to sit still and listen. They want to experiment with stuff, move stuff around, and find solutions for themselves. Truthfully, grown men don't readily give up this part of who they are. Hence, if a man is lost, asking for directions is like admitting defeat. *Ha! He had to ask for assistance. He couldn't figure it out for himself. How humiliating!* That is how we think.

Men want to win. Men want to emerge victorious. Men want to be

effective. We will be a lone ranger, if need be. If you find an individual needing guidance, don't get him off track by discussing the problem; especially if you are suggesting a solution that seems perfectly logical to you but goes against his grain. If you pressure him to do it the 'logical' way, do not be surprised if instead of thanking you, he brusquely tells you to back off and leave him alone.

Men want to be strong. As mentioned, men do not want to be told

what to do. "Read a self-help book," a friend suggests. "Nah," we say under our breath. It will make us feel vulnerable, right? It will tell us what we're doing wrong. It will tell us how to do things differently. Who needs a book like that? We've gotten along just fine in life. Why change? It is better to just suck it up and let people's complaints roll off our backs. Maybe if we let enough time pass, things will get better on its own. Or so we hope.

I don't know about you, but this way of thinking is a bit absurd. God teaches us differently. God *wants* us to ask. How can one receive if one does not ask? The reason God teaches us to ask is so we can learn to receive. We need to understand the humble concept of, "We have not because we ask not." God promises us so many things in His word. Here are just a few from the New International Version:

1. **Mark 11:24** – "Therefore I tell you, whatever you *ask* for in prayer, believe that you have received it, and it will be yours."

2. **John 14:13-14** – "And I will do whatever you *ask* in my name, so that the Father may be glorified in the Son. You may *ask* me for anything in my name, and I will do it."

3. **James 1:6-7** – "But when you *ask*, you must believe and not doubt, because the one who doubts is like a wave of the sea, blown and tossed by the wind. That person should not expect to receive anything from the Lord."

4. **John 15:16** – "You did not choose me, but I chose you and appointed you so that you might go and bear fruit—fruit that will last—and so that whatever you *ask* in my name the Father will give you.

5. 1 John 5:14-15 – "This is the confidence we have in approaching God: that if we *ask* anything according to his will, he hears us. And if we know that he hears us—whatever we *ask*—we know that we have what we *asked* of him."

Now, I know a lot of you reading this might have already learned the importance of asking, or are learning how important it is. Hopefully you're helping other men learn the same. Asking reveals our humility, strength and wisdom. Asking God shows that you surrender to Him in order to get the much needed answers to everything. When I think about it, growing up the way I did should have taught me these things. But I wasn't able to see the value in asking so I became defiant. It doesn't matter the other person's motive behind why they want you to ask, because it's not about them. It's about you!

Growing up in my household, it should have been about my siblings and I learning how to be humble; unfortunately, it wasn't taught or explained. Lucky for you, I have a whole chapter set aside on the subject of being humble. To ask something of someone requires faith, especially if you are asking God for it. Faith is another great subject that is set aside for us to talk about. I have discovered that sometimes in life we get frustrated and even upset with God about something. Ok, that happens to the best of us. What do you do about it, though? Do you just stay upset at God and let it fester inside or do you draw closer to God and seek answers?

Scripture tells us plainly in the book of James:

"You do not have because you do not ask God. When you ask, you do not receive, because you ask with wrong motives, that you may spend what you get on your pleasures." (v4:2-3)

Have you ever thought about that? You don't have because you don't ASK. The verse goes on to further say, when you do ask, you don't receive, because you ask with wrong motives. That is so important to understand. Not only is asking God essential, but so are our motives behind asking. Why do you want that promotion at work? Why do you want that new car? Why do you want a bigger house? Why do you want to have a ministry? The reason why is just as important as asking in the first place.

What I've come to learn and understand is this: before we ask for anything, our motives should line up with God's standard. You see, what happens is that we ask God for something or about something and we don't get the answer that we want. Did you get that? We don't get the answer that WE want. That is a huge problem when following Christ. Until we learn that God isn't some kind of wishing well or fulfillment center we will never have or receive all that He has in store for us.

Our wants and desires have got to be in line with God's initial plans for us. That is how He answers prayer. If something we ask for doesn't happen, it doesn't mean necessarily that you haven't prayed enough or served enough. It could simply mean that it wasn't the right thing for us. Don't get upset with God. Don't pout and start believing that God doesn't love you or care about you.

Think of it like this: **God knows what is best.**

Some of us may even do this with our own children. We tell them they can't have something or do something because it would not be good for them. Why? Because we as parents know better from experience. God is the same way. His thoughts are not our thoughts. His ways are higher than our ways. God knows what is best for us because He created us. He is our Maker! If anything, ask Him which way to go, or when to move. I believe He will show you. Whatever the situation, God knows best.

A couple of years ago, my wife, Carrie and I wanted to move to Stone Mountain, Georgia. We lived a few cities away in Lawrenceville, but we loved going to Stone Mountain during the middle of the week for date nights. For a while, taking our fold-up chairs and sitting lakeside at our special spot with Subway bags in hand was the best. Other times, Carrie and I would walk, jog, or even ride our bikes around the huge 1,686 foot mountain. Anyway, after we started talking about possibly moving to the city of Stone Mountain, we began to pray about it and after a short time, we found a house in a very nice neighborhood that would be ideal. We met with the landlord and fell in love with the house. It had 5-bedrooms with a fenced-in backyard and even an office. The plan was for each of the kids to have their own bedroom. After one conversation with the landlord, he leased the house to us. We were elated. We moved in a couple of weeks later.

During our stay there, our oldest daughter, who was 21 at the time, moved out regardless of her commitment to stay there for three years. That meant her part of the rent was now gone. But God actually had a plan that none of us could have foreseen. We were able to help out a few different men at various times by renting out the room for cheap. We had taken in other people before at our previous house, so doing it again was okay with us.

The following year we fell on very hard times. I lost my job and so we began falling behind on the rent. We spoke with our landlord regularly about our situation. He actually allowed us a grace period where we didn't have to pay any rent at all! This was supposed to be until I got another job. Well guess what? I never got another job! I did, however, start receiving unemployment checks, which still weren't enough to cover the full rent after the grace period was up. Even with everyone pitching in, we were only able to come up with half of the rent on a regular basis. This went on for another 2 years! Finally, after my unemployment ran out and I still didn't have a job, we needed to do something.

The company Carrie worked for began to down-size and the future of her position was not as bright as she had once hoped. Things were ripping apart at the seams and we felt pressured to do something. Carrie found another position in Myrtle Beach, South Carolina. My boys, who were all of age, had a few plans of their own. This position seemed to fit the path that she wanted to take in her career and I too thought about a fresh start with my career. I wanted to get back involved with Connection Leadership, a motivational company I had launched and doing something with MAN ON PURPOSE was on my heart as well.

Everything happened so fast. Carrie got the job in Myrtle Beach making more than she was in Atlanta. We thought this was our way out! It was a fresh, new start. Within two weeks, everything was complete. I had taken Carrie to South Carolina a week prior and I began clearing the house and putting things into storage. We were all excited! We took only what we could carry in our small SUV.

Now, did God tell us to move to Myrtle Beach? Did we take any time to consult Him? We started asking these questions shortly after we had already moved there. Neither Carrie nor I voiced this to each other. It wasn't until much later that we told each other that we think we made a huge mistake. You see, here's why. Remember our landlord? Although our lease was up, we left him and his family in severe debt with the house. They were trying to help us. They had to borrow money just to keep their rental property from falling into foreclosure. By good faith, they blessed us by allowing us move in with no credit check, no references, nothing. God allowed the landlord to be a blessing, but we didn't return the blessing by being responsible stewards.

For whatever the reason, we did not seek God in our move to Myrtle Beach. In turn we caused harm to another family. Learning to be a family of integrity, of course we made small payments here and there to help, but the damage had been already done. Yes, the housing market crashing caused his house to lose value, but nothing could have been done to keep the house. What matters is that we didn't let God sort through everything and lay our concerns at His feet. We took it upon ourselves and made the decision to move. Our decision caused someone to lose their house.

It wasn't until recently that I received this epiphany. Carrie and I talked pretty deep about it. I tell you this story to shed light on how important it is to ensure that you *ask* God about everything. Not only was there the situation with the house, but we left our church too. At the time, the only church family I had was right there. I got saved there. I got baptized there. Carrie and I were involved in various ministries there. MAN ON PURPOSE was actually doing better there than I had realized. It was like we pulled one rock and the whole structure collapsed. I'm not kidding.

Since our move, Carrie and I have struggled big time trying to find where God wants us to be here in Myrtle Beach. We are constantly asking God all kinds of questions trying to get back on track. His way, not our way. I believe He has already forgiven us, because we asked Him for His forgiveness. Now, I am so cautious to make sure I ask Him, not just daily, but multiple times a day for His guidance and His direction. I'm not gun shy; I have just gotten to the point where I understand that none of this will work without asking God first. After I ask I must then listen and obey what He says to do.

Men, it gets us absolutely nowhere when we try and make decisions on our own. Throughout the years, after making so many mistakes such as the one I just shared with you, I am just tired and weary. I so desire to live out my purpose and I believe the only way to do so begins with ASKING God. If you read and know the Bible, then you agree that the greatest leaders sought God's guidance in all things, and when they didn't seek Him, there were always repercussions.

The Bible reminds us that in our weakness, God is strong. 2 Corinthians 12:10 says it this way:

"That is why, for Christ's sake, I delight in weaknesses, in insults, in hardships, in persecutions, in difficulties. For when I am weak, then I am strong."

God's strength is the ultimate strength. God's knowledge is the ultimate knowledge. God's direction is the ultimate destination. When you believe that His answer to your question is truth, you cannot get lost on this journey. All you have to do is stop, and step into Him to get the answers. Go ahead, I dare you to ask Him! When you do, watch what unfolds before you!

MY PRAYER:

Heavenly Father, I want to take this moment to thank You for this opportunity of writing this book. I believe each and every topic has come directly from You. These are but a few topics that so many of us men need to get inside of us and practice. As we have just finished the very first topic - ASK, I pray that what is written and what has been read would touch the lives of countless men, empowering them to come to You first and foremost. May they ask those important and often time insignificant questions and requests. I pray that any spirit of fear or pride would be overcome in the name of Jesus. I thank You, Lord that we are able to come to You in prayer, to not only lay our requests before You, but also to receive Your strength of humility and ask others for help in situations where help is needed.

Thank You, heavenly Father.
In Jesus' name, AMEN!

CHAPTER 2

BELIEVE

2

B

"Therefore I tell you, whatever you ask for in prayer, believe that you have received it, and it will be yours." (Mark 11:24)

In the first chapter, we learned that asking is the first thing we need to do to become the man we are intended to be with purpose, on purpose. At the very end of the chapter I wrote that all the asking in the world won't help unless… Unless what? Unless you BELIEVE!

Just like asking God for something takes faith, so does believing God for something. Did you know that your faith is fueled by what you believe? You have to believe that God will do what you are asking and praying for. It's not about if He can do it, because God can do anything He wants. You see, if your request lines up with the will of God, then there can be no

doubt that God can and will grant what you have asked of Him.
James chapter 2 says it quite well.

"But someone will say, 'You have faith, and I have works.' Show me your faith without your works, and I will show you my faith by my works. You believe that there is one God. You do well. Even the demons believe— and tremble! But do you want to know, O foolish man, that faith without works is dead? Was not Abraham our father justified by works when he offered Isaac his son on the altar? Do you see that faith was working together with his works, and by works faith was made perfect? And the Scripture was fulfilled which says, <u>'Abraham believed God</u>, and it was accounted to him for righteousness.' And he was called the friend of God. You see then that a man is justified by works, and not by faith only" (v18-24).

If I came to you and told you that 2+2=4 you would believe me and agree, right? That's because we have learned that equation as a child and we know that the answer is correct. That's easy. Well what if I told you that God wants you to be that confident in everything that has to do with Him. It's true. What? Now you don't *believe* me? Just as the equation has been proven to you, so has God proven Himself to be who He says He is. If you say you love God and are a Christ follower, then there can be no doubt, just like there is no doubt that 2+2=4.

God, our Creator says He has a plan and a purpose for our lives, do you believe that? How does one get to a point where they "believe" something? According to the dictionary, to believe means: to have confidence in the truth, the existence, or the reliability of somet hing, although without absolute proof that one is right in doing so:

"Only if one believes in something can one act purposefully."

— Joshua Keene

According to this definition, the math example I gave is based off something that has been proven and leaves no room for doubt. Whereas this definition says, "One doesn't need absolute proof to believe something; you only need to be confident in the truth." So as with God, both definitions apply and I "believe". Our absolute proof is called God's Word. His character will not allow Him to lie. God cannot lie!

I must inform you that I am not writing this book to convince anyone of His existence. I am writing this with the expectation that all who read this book already "believe" that God is truth. Only God Himself can bring clarity to someone's mind or convince them of His existence.

Mark 9:22-24 shares a conversation that Jesus is having with a father concerning his son who is possessed by an evil spirit. The father says: "But if you can do anything, take pity on us and help us." "If you *can*?" said Jesus (emphasis added). "Everything is possible for one who believes." Immediately the boy's father exclaimed, "I do believe; help me overcome my unbelief!"

According to this scripture, Jesus says, "Everything is possible for one who believes." What an amazing promise! But what does it really mean? Spiritual maturity teaches us that "everything" is different for each of us.

"Therefore, if anyone is in Christ, the new creation has come: The old has gone, the new is here." (2 Corinthians 5:17)

What this is saying is that once we've given our lives over to God we begin to change. God works in us by the Holy Spirit to transform us into new men. Our thinking changes and we don't have the same desires or wants that we used to have. We begin to live more for Him than for ourselves. God begins to open up different opportunities for us. We find ourselves thinking and doing things that we never could have imagined. God begins to be the number one focus in our lives, which means doing all that is asked of us by Him.

Now, the previous statement that Jesus made becomes clear. Everything is possible for one who believes is indeed true because now our "everything" is God related. Anything that lines up with God's will for you, He will give to you. At this point, you aren't going to go into prayer and ask your Creator for frivolous things. No, you're going to ask Him for things that are Kingdom related.

To believe in Christ is to act on Christ's behalf. Do you just believe or do you **believe** with every fiber in your body? Having a strong belief in something can carry us pretty far. A strong belief in something can have us do things that we never thought possible. Believing in something requires some sort of action. Abraham had faith in God yes, but he also needed to believe God at His word, and because he believed, God counted that as righteousness to him. Now, don't get faith confused with believe. We will discuss faith a little later on; as a matter of fact, that is the "F" in our ABC's.

Throughout history we know of individuals who have had beliefs which ultimately led to their deaths. Probably the most important story of all time is when Jesus Christ sacrificed His life for all of us to redeem us for our sins. Jesus believed that by sacrificing Himself, we would have an opportunity to live with Him for eternity. For 33 years, Jesus walked the earth humbly and focused on heaven's purpose here on earth. He did what He needed to do while He was here and then left. Satan tried to tempt Him and get Him off His mission, but Jesus remained true and stayed focused on things above, not on earthly things. All because He believed.

Billy Graham, a great man of God, had to believe in something greater than himself as well. He was a true believer of Christ and he lived his life accordingly. Everything he did was to further God's Kingdom; not his own. Because of that, God used him greatly. Billy Graham once turned down a five-year, five-million-dollar contract offered to him from NBC because he had prior commitments during his touring revivals. Talk about being focused…Because he *believed*, God has used him greatly.

Men, we cannot just believe God, we have to *believe in* Him also. It's very much like you need to love your wife, but you also need to be *in love* with her. Maybe that will help. Did you know that the word "believe" in the Bible means more than simply agreeing in our minds that something might be true? It also means to "trust"! It means that we are to believe so strongly in God that we are willing to commit our lives to Him and live the way we know He wants us to live.

Suppose you were walking along a path and you came to a bridge, which crossed a deep canyon. You might look at it and believe that it would hold your weight, and you might even see other people walking across it confirming that it is holding their weight. But so far, your "belief" in the bridge remains in your head. When do you really believe that the bridge will hold you? I know you know it... When you are willing to sacrifice your life and actually walk across it.

It is the same way with Christ. Yes, we can believe that God exists, but God wants us to come to know Him personally. And He has bridged the gap between us by sending His Son to remove the barrier of sin and become that "bridge." To believe in Christ is to commit our lives by faith to Christ— to trust Him personally as our Lord and Savior.

Again, I remind you of the scripture where it says, "Faith without works is dead". To end this chapter, let me ask you a final question: if you were arrested for being a Christian, would there be enough evidence to convict you? You say you believe, so what are you doing to show evidence of that?

I recall March 22, 2015 when Carrie and I went to the movie theatre to watch "Do You Believe". If you have not seen it yet, I suggest you do. The obvious question that was asked in the movie was this: Do you believe? If you answered yes to that question, then the next question is this: What are you doing about it?

"Very truly I tell you, whoever believes in me will do the works I have been doing, and they will do even greater things than these, because I am going to the Father. And I will do whatever you ask in my name, so that the Father may be glorified in the Son. You may ask me for anything in my name, and I will do it." (John 14:12-14)

No one can force you to do either of the first two topics in this book. To *ask* is a choice and to *believe* is a choice. I pray that you are still with me as we continue on our journey together. Like I just mentioned, not only are the topics your choice, but so is every other principal we will be discussing in this book. I am *asking* you to continue on with the *belief* that you will get what God wants you to get out of this; but again... it is your *choice*.

MY PRAYER: Heavenly Father, I do believe; help me

overcome my unbelief! I pray this for all the men, Lord. Christianity today seems to be lacking the power to transform lives completely. I believe one of the reasons for this is because of our lack of really believing in You with our whole being. So many of us say we believe, but there is no evidence of that belief. It is as though a lot of us are merely "just believing" and adding to the worldly things, but this is not what You want. Lord, please help us to receive You completely so that our belief is so uncontrollably strong that others will want to believe in You as well. Help us to develop all that is necessary to have such a belief in You that the things of the world will not even matter. Believing in You is living for You, and if necessary, dying for You just as Jesus did for all of us. Lord, we do believe; help us overcome our unbelief!

Thank You, Father.

In Jesus' name, AMEN!

CHAPTER ③

CHOOSE ©

"Although the Lord gives you the bread of adversity and the water of affliction, your teachers will be hidden no more; with your own eyes you will see them. Whether you turn to the right or to the left, your ears will hear a voice behind you, saying, 'This is the way; walk in it."

(Isaiah 30:20, 21)

Which way do I go? What do I say? What do I wear? What am I going to eat? Where am I going to park? What day should I schedule my appointment for and what time? Paper or plastic? To be or not to be? Oh my gosh! So many decisions to make from so many choices.

Everything today has a choice attached to it. You can choose from different colors, to different brands, to different tastes, and the list goes on and on. How do you choose? What method do you choose by? Have you ever made the wrong choice? I'm sure all of us have made a few wrong choices in life. In chapter one, I shared with you a situation where I believe I made a wrong choice. I can surely tell you about many more bad choices I have made throughout my life. Bad choice after bad choice. Can you relate?

Are you familiar with the Bible story in Joshua where he has the people assembled and he has to remind the Israelites of the many things that God has done for them because of their false idol worship. Indeed, God was pretty upset with them. The Israelites had to make a choice. Let's see what Joshua says in chapter 24, verse 15:

"But if serving the Lord seems undesirable to you, then choose for yourselves this day whom you will serve, whether the gods your ancestors served beyond the Euphrates, or the gods of the Amorites, in whose land you are living. But as for me and my household, we will serve the Lord."

The Israelites made a covenant with God to serve only Him and they chose right. Joshua and his family chose correctly from the beginning but most of them just needed a strong reminder. There are so many accounts in the Bible of powerful men simply making bad choices. However, there are also quite a few who made good choices, and they received God's reward for doing so. But the first bad choice recorded in Scripture, the one that was heard around the world and the one that we are all still paying for was committed by the first humans, Adam & Eve.

Oh, brother. Really, these two had it made. They could have had everything. Everything! All they had to do was leave one tree alone. They could have had all the other thousand or so trees, but no, they had to choose the one that God commanded them not to eat from. The first bad choice went very wrong and it cost them their life. But if serving the Lord seems undesirable to you, then **choose** for yourselves this day whom you will serve, whether the gods of your ancestors or the gods who are in the land you are living. But as for me and my household, we will serve the Lord.

We are a people who are in need of God. He created us that way. His desire has always been for us to choose Him. Look around at how many other gods are out there *trying* to take the place of the one and only true God. We make things like sports into a God. We make money into a God. We allow greed and materialism to be a God. Anything that consumes our thinking, our time, and our income becomes a God to us, and we render service to it. We chase after it as if our lives depended on it. It is like that "thing" has become our God.

One thing I have learned is this: You cannot say that you love and serve God when that "thing" you keep chasing is first and foremost in your heart. You cannot chase after God and be scooping up loads of cash along the way. Either you choose for God to be first and foremost in your life or you choose to do this life on your own (because after all you are a very smart and intelligent human being and you don't need someone telling you how to live). If we are so smart, then why do we have other gods in our life telling us what to do all the time?

We all answer to "a god" one way or another. I don't know about you, but for me, it just makes sense to choose "the real God" to answer to. He's the One that promises everlasting life so why would I choose a god that will lead me on and then when there is no more left I am deserted and left helpless and hopeless. God is the only One that makes promises and backs them up with truth. The One who created you and me is the only One that can do that. The One that knows us better than we know ourselves is the only One that can promise all that His Word can give.

"No one can serve two masters. Either you will hate the one and love the other, or you will be devoted to the one and despise the other. You cannot serve both God and money." (Matthew 6:24)

It's one or the other! This requires us to make a choice. The day I chose to give my life to God was the best decision I remember ever making in my life. I didn't even think it through. I had no idea what was in store for me. I just said it and then I did it! And yeah, I said it alright.

On one particular Saturday, still living in Georgia, Carrie and I had been fighting off and on all day. There we were, not married, but living together with her four kids, shouting back and forth. As much as we fought back then, I don't even know how on earth we stayed together. By early evening something snapped in me and I blurted out, "That's it!

We are going to #&*! %&#@ church!" I don't even know why that came out of my mouth because I had never really been to church before. I was a Jehovah's Witness for a few years as a kid, but I didn't know anything about any church.

Sunday morning came and we all got dressed and off we went. *Where am I going?* I thought to myself getting into the car. About 30 minutes later we ended up at Victory World Church in Norcross. We were even on time! I parked and we entered. I had no idea how profound my choice would be over the next several years.

While we were there I thought to myself, *Yes! We found "the place".* But then it hit me, we didn't find anything. I now believe because I made a choice, God led us there. Let me explain a little more. You see, without my knowledge, Carrie had been in touch with a woman named Deborah Turner there at the church. Because of everything I was putting her through, my wife needed to reach out to someone, somewhere. She had been talking to Deborah for a couple of months, unbeknownst to me, and on the day we were driving to church, Carrie was praying that we would end up at Victory and we did!

This is one example of many that proves when we choose God, He always comes through. Let me repeat that, when you choose God, He always comes through. He does and He has, because His name is Faithful. We only need to make that choice to serve Him. He knows all the worldly things that are battling for positions in our lives. But the great thing about God is that He honors His Word, especially to those who choose Him over everything else. The way God does things may not always turn out how we think they should, but then we must remind ourselves what the Bible says.

"As the heavens are higher than the earth, so are my ways higher than your ways and my thoughts than your thoughts." (Isaiah 55:9)

Choices are the foundation of our lives. The choices you, I and someone else will make ultimately determines the direction our life will go. The choice you make today can have a profound effect on your life and others as quick right now and as far down the road as five or more years. You and I cannot possibly see that far into our future. Well, at least I know I can't see that far. I do know who can though. My Creator can.

Why is it so important for us to have a relationship with God? So He can guide us in the right direction. But first, we must choose Him over everything else. I'm not saying that you can't have and do things, but the attention you give those things should be done in moderation. In order for our lives to play out the way God intended them to, there has to be a proper balance.

So many people complain about the cards they have been dealt and how much they want to give them back to the dealer. You see, what often times happens in life is we look over at our neighbor or see someone at our job, and we look at our "hand" saying to ourselves, *Their "hand" is better than ours.* We then figure out ways to get that other person's "hand". When we think like this, we only see the present. We don't even think about how they got their "hand". What if they've been cheating in life? What if someone else gave them their "hand"? There are just too many parameters and too many unknowns.

You must realize that you cannot live someone else's life. You have to choose to live the life that you have been given. God did not fearfully and wonderfully create each of us simply to work a job and put bread on the table. I believe that is a chicken man's answer. God created you and me to do incredible things here on earth, and even more incredible things to further His Kingdom. In order to do that, you have got to break out of the worldly mold and choose to exercise faith in God. He will guide you to become the man you are intended to be.

I believe more men now than ever are living "pretend" lives. I know I sure did for a long time. I was lost and could not figure out who I was. I had put on so many different masks and played so many different roles in life that I simply got lost. The choices I made kept backfiring and I could not figure out why. I believe God was trying to show me my real identity, but I kept running away.

I'll say it like this: if I made 1,000 choices, 900 of them were bad ones. No, really. Actually it might even be closer to 950. So, what did I do with all these bad choices? I learned that God can take all of the bad choices I have ever made and use them to benefit others as well as bring glory to

His name. Amazing... The Word says,

"And we know that in all things God works for the good of those who love him, who have been called according to his purpose."

(Romans 8:28)

No matter the circumstance, the situation, or even the bad choices that you have made, God can turn it all around and use it for good. You see God does not waste anything. I believe that even if one chooses to live their life according to their own way and later chooses to serve God, that person's past does not go to waste. God can and will use it for good. Don't get so down on yourself. Take your concerns to God and ask Him before you make a choice. If you are wondering what to do now that you've already made a bad choice, take that to Him also. He can turn you around, right where you are standing.

As I write this book, my wife and I will have to make a choice to move again soon. We know that coming to Myrtle Beach was a bad choice for us, although God turned it around so that it wasn't a disaster. We made a bad choice and we went to God and repented for not seeking His direction on what we should have done and God has forgiven us. He will put us back on track.

Now, I certainly cannot see my family ending up back in Stone Mountain where we left off, but we are dedicated to God's guidance. He'll have us where we need to be. I can be confident of this truth. The biggest choice we have to make at this moment in our life is choosing to follow God's prompting of where we need to go. It doesn't matter if it makes sense to us. It doesn't matter whether we like that location or not. However we think or feel about what we believe to be God's decision doesn't matter. The only thing that matters is doing what God wants us to do. Carrie and I can only see so far, and even if we were blind, that wouldn't matter either. We believe, trust, and have faith in knowing that God knows the way and will never lead us wrong. The Bible says:

"Many are the plans in a person's heart, but it is the Lord's purpose that prevails." (Proverbs 19:21)

I encourage you to read the Bible and see some of the bad choices that history's greatest leaders have made. You'll find that what caused them to make those bad choices in the first place was often times their PRIDE. There goes that oh so ugly word again. Pride is the root of a lot of stupid things we do as men. Pride is definitely a hindrance in asking God for help and it is a hindrance in believing any of God's promises too. It ranks as probably the number one reason we make poor or bad choices. I know that's where I was at one time, for sure.

Thinking about it, my pride has kept me from and gotten me into so much. My stupid pride almost got me shot once. Seriously. One time I had a rookie cop pull a gun on me because I was walking toward him. The other two officers pulled their guns as well. All this happened because of my 250 pound bouncer-looking-self would not get down on the ground when I was told to. This of course, was long ago. I have since learned that pride does not pay. It just doesn't. I was going to insert a couple of scriptures on pride right here, but I found something interesting that I want to share before I insert them.

Here's a list of behaviors that can tell you if there is a hint of pride in you. From this list, I realized that I still have pride issues that I'm going to have to work on. I'm not going to explain any of these because then this chapter would be about pride. I just want to make you aware of them so that you can pray and let God open your eyes to whether or not you have some pride issues to work out, as I surely do. Pride is probably the major reason for a lack of favor with God and therefore lack of success in ministry. It is also the major root issue in failure.

The list includes, but is not limited to: **insecurity, the need to be right, being argumentative, more invested in being heard than in hearing, anger, irritability and impatience, lacking submissive attitude, not easily corrected, receiving correction but not changing, needing others to take your advice, needing to proclaim your titles or degrees, being stubborn, and lastly comparing and competing.**

How many of these do you still struggle with? I listed them because if you are making bad choices and can't figure out why, then maybe some of the listed issues are the reasons why. I mean if you are seeking God for help with your choices and you are argumentative or lacking a submissive attitude, you are not going to hear a word that He is saying. It all starts with the "MAN IN THE MIRROR" – YOU!

Regardless if it is I, you, or we… being honest with ourselves and giving these issues to God needs to happen. We need to ask Him for help to make the necessary changes, and then patiently wait on Him to do it. Meanwhile, write these issues down and take them with you to a close friend, or your men's group or your small group and ask them which one of these they see in you. When you do, ask someone for accountability to begin the process of change. As I mentioned, I'm going to have to work on a couple of these myself. I'll be praying for you guys and I hope you'll do the same for me. That is why Scripture says this:

"But God gives us more grace… He opposes the proud but shows favor to the humble." (James 4:6)

"Pride goes before destruction; a haughty spirit before a fall."

(Proverbs 16:18)

What choices do you have to make today or tomorrow? Are you going to ask God first before making them? It's a choice! What you choose today can have long term effects on more people than you can imagine. You cannot, even in your great educated mind, begin to see every single consequence or benefit your choice may have; good or bad. That is why I put my trust in the One who can. No horoscope, no palm reader, no muse, and definitely no dead fat man statues! His name is Jehovah. He is alive and He is our Creator.

MY PRAYER: Heavenly Father, making good choices seems to be so hard in today's society. As men, we just don't make right choices for ourselves, but all those connected to us. Lord, my prayer is that men would give up trying to make these choices themselves and come to You in prayer and wait to hear Your answer. You know the plans and direction we should go in because You made us! Help us Lord to not be so prideful making choices on our own. Your desire is for us to come to You and ask for direction and guidance. When we seek You, our Creator, for leadership concerning our difficult choices - that is wisdom! I pray that men everywhere would first and foremost choose You over everything else that is trying to lure them away. In order to be truly fulfilled in this life, we have got to make the most important decision our most important choice, which is love You and serve You wholeheartedly with everything we are and with everything we have.

In Jesus' name, AMEN!

CHAPTER 4
DO

Do not merely listen to the word, and so deceive yourselves. Do what it says. (James 1:22)

The second part of this Bible verse tells us to "*Do* what it says". To *do* something requires action. Here are a few definitions of the word 'do' taken from Dictionary.com:

1. To perform (an act, duty, role, etc.)
2. To execute (a piece or amount of work)
3. To put forth; exert

Do means to accomplish, achieve, and bring action to an end or a conclusion. Accomplish and achieve bother mean successful completion of an undertaking. Accomplish emphasizes attaining a desired goal through effort, skill, and perseverance: *to accomplish what one has hoped for.* Achieve emphasizes accomplishing something important, excellent, or great: to achieve a major breakthrough.

So far we have covered – Ask, Believe, and Choose. Each one of these requires us to Do. After reading this book, the goal is to bring yourself to *do.* Why am I making such a big deal about this small, two letter word? Because, this tiny, two letter word carries a huge punch. Everything that I am writing in this book requires us to *do.* For most of our life, if not all of our life, we *have* to do. If this little word weren't such a powerful word, then why would NIKE have used the slogan, "Just Do It"? Take a look at the rest of the passage in James chapter one:

"Do not merely listen to the word, and so deceive yourselves. Do what it says. Anyone who listens to the word but does not do what it says is like someone who looks at his face in a mirror and, after looking at himself, goes away and immediately forgets what he looks like. But whoever looks intently into the perfect law that gives freedom, and continues in it—not forgetting what they have heard, but doing it—they will be blessed in what they do." (James 1:22-27)

We have been given a directive to not merely listen to the Word, but we have to *do* what it says. It didn't say anything about doing what God's Word says after your situation gets better, or when you have transportation, or when you buy the right outfit, or when your wife does what she's supposed to do, or when you get a raise. You get the picture. Why do we always seem to have an excuse when it comes to the doing part? I will never know. Let's just stay at home and watch the church service from the convenience of our warm and soft Lazy Boy sofas, you know. But wait... What does the Bible say?

"Let us consider… not giving up meeting together, as some are in the habit of doing, but encouraging one another—and all the more as you see the Day approaching." (Hebrews 10:24-25)

There are plenty of *do's* in the Bible as well as *do not's*, and both of them are important to our welfare and our service to God. It is God who gives us these do's and do not's for our own good. You may ask yourself, "How can I become the man God intended me to be with purpose, on purpose?" It's pretty simple. "Do not merely listen to the Word and deceive yourselves. Do what it says". How about this verse from Romans 12:2:

"Do not conform to the pattern of this world, but be transformed by the renewing of your mind. Then you will be able to test and approve what God's will is—his good, pleasing and perfect will."

Are you conforming to the patterns of the world? I know you've heard it a thousand times. Are you partially conforming to the patterns of the world? This verse has double action going on. If we do not conform to the patterns of the world, we can be transformed by the renewing of our minds. Don't conform, but transform! All this verse is really saying is that we should not be following the world as our example. And I agree.

I know this scripture has been debated to death about what is allowed and what is not allowed, but I don't see where this is an issue. It's pretty clear to me. I am not to follow what the world is doing. If the world is covering their bodies with tattoos, it makes sense that we shouldn't be. If the world is allowing and participating in abortions, it makes sense that we shouldn't be. If the world is engaging in adultery, it makes sense that we shouldn't be. If the world is caught up in greed, I don't even need to finish my line, because you get the point.

If we are allowing our minds to be renewed, then we wouldn't be thinking or even trying to justify what is okay or not. The renewing of our mind means that we are in line with God's will and how He thinks. All of the worldly things are obsolete. There would be no need to debate God's Word or to try and find loopholes in it. Only someone trying to hold on to something worldly would think it's acceptable to bend Scripture.

I know for a fact that you do not need to be "tatted" out to reach the lost. You do not need to create your own identity to talk about Jesus. The power of God's Word is not based on what your hairstyle is or what kind of jeans you are wearing, and especially not the amount of tattoos or piercings you have. The power of Christ comes through regardless of any of that. I believe, as men, we only do those things because we want to hold on to some sort of identity and self-preservation. We are supposed to be different in the world because God's light shines through us. Jesus and many after Jesus have stayed true to who they are in God and that is what transforms people. You need only to do what God's Word says to do and dare to be who God created you to be; not who you are trying to create.

Truthfully speaking, we do not need to *fit in* in order to do. By no means am I judging or condemning anyone, because I too have fallen prey to Satan's lies. I have a permanent tattoo on my arm. I was close to getting more until I grabbed a hold of God's input. I share this, not to debate whether tattoos are okay or not, but whether we as Christians are participating in the same things that the world is. Perhaps, instead of us jumping the gun and making these kinds of decisions on our own, we really need to consult God. Since God is the creator of each and every one of us, don't you think He knows how He wants His children to look?

Everything the world can offer us is not all from God. It's like an artist painting a canvas and having someone come along and take the brush out of the artist's hand and paint over the original painting. God is the artist of this beautiful world and he painted everything in it, including mankind. But what we've done is added to His work without consulting Him. Have you consulted God lately? Particularly on how He wants you to look or what He wants you to do with your life? The Message version says it this way:

"Don't become so well-adjusted to your culture that you fit into it without even thinking. Instead, fix your attention on God. You'll be changed from the inside out. Readily recognize what he wants from you, and quickly respond to it. Unlike the culture around you, always dragging you down to its level of immaturity, God brings the best out of you, develops well-formed maturity in you." **(Romans 12:2 MSG)**

Wow! **This all begins with the renewing of our mind.** But to get to this point with God you need to *do* God's word. You have got to *do* prayer. You have got to *do* and not merely listen. I liken the word *do* with being obedient. It's like this: to do is to be obedient, to be obedient requires us to do. Does this make sense? Look at this verse:

"So I say, walk by the Spirit, and you will not gratify the desires of the flesh. For the flesh desires what is contrary to the Spirit and the Spirit what is contrary to the flesh. They are in conflict with each other, so that you are not to do whatever you want. But if you are led by the Spirit, you are not under the law." (Galatians 5:16-18)

This is why I know that all this worldly stuff is not to be a part of our lives, because there is a *do* here. We are to walk by the spirit. That means we are supposed to be letting God pour into us through the Holy Spirit, which in turn, leads us and guides us through all the messiness of life. *If* we are truly walking in the spirit, like we are supposed to be, then our televisions would be off most of the time. Walking in the spirit would have us refraining from posting junk on Facebook or other social media outlets. We would be able to control the urges of our bodies instead of our bodies controlling us. Here's a tough pill to swallow – guys, we would be able to control how we look at women if we were walking in the spirit and not in the flesh.

Ouch. I know. The flesh wants to do all the things that are not good for us. The flesh wants us to look, dress, and talk a certain way to fit into society, but the Holy Spirit doesn't want that. He could care less about fitting in because the Holy Spirit is God Himself. One of our duties as Christians is to let the Holy Spirit lead us. Verse 24 in Galatians chapter 5 states, "Those who belong to Christ Jesus have crucified the flesh with its passions and desires." Not our desires, not our passions. Those are of the flesh, which we are to crucify so that we can be transformed by the renewing of our minds, which in turn makes us new creations in Christ.

"Therefore, if anyone is in Christ, the new creation has come: The old has gone, the new is here!" (2 Corinthians 5:17)

Ok, you might be wondering, "How do we achieve everything that God requires us to do? Well, the only way I can answer that is by pointing you right back to Scripture. In chapter 4 of Philippians, Paul is writing to the Philippi Church and in verse 12 he talks about being content in every situation. In verse 13 he admits to only being able to do so through Christ who gives him the strength.

"I can do all things through him who gives me strength."

(Philippians 4:13)

Outside of God, you can't and I can't do this. What we *can* do is let God work in us and give us the strength to *do* what He requires us to do. You see that? Full dependency. We do this through prayer and having a relationship with Him. That's what it's all about.

This book I am writing is only because God prompted me to do so. I can tell you right now that I have attempted to write this book that you are reading quite a few times. Each time I started, I could never get past the first chapter. It wasn't until I made the decision to fast and pray, and press into God's presence that I was able to write this book to completion. For three full days, I have committed myself to writing, spending time in prayer, and worshiping. I believe, being obedient to God's voice has allowed Him to work in me so that He will be glorified.

Now, I am not saying that I completed this book in three days, but I am saying that the three days became a springboard to its completion. You see, I knew from a while ago that I was supposed to write a book; I just didn't know when or how to go about doing so. That's why I didn't do it before. For so long, I was trying to do it on my own timing and in my own ability. But I have since learned that God's perfect will cannot be accomplished unless it is done on His time and with His ability so I do don't boast about what *I* accomplished. I believe I am in the midst of doing God's will right now. I believe this moment is the right time for you to be reading these very words. I know this because when I fasted for 21 days, I received direction and saw what I needed to do so this moment could be possible.

I remember at the time of my fast, I had been working on another project that would have turned into a business, but I knew that something wasn't right. This endeavor would have taken too much time away from what was really important. What's really important to me is helping guys just like you take this journey; the same journey that I am on. I believe God wants to do great things with MAN ON PURPOSE and I want to be on board.

For a short moment, I had stepped down from MAN ON PURPOSE to get on track with God so He could lead the ministry. I wanted MAN ON PURPOSE to be as effective as possible; empowering men to become the men they are intended to be with purpose, on purpose. I was struggling with some things and I needed to put myself in the proper place so God could work through me. I know for a fact that if God isn't in front of the ministry, then it won't do what it was designed to do. It was during my fast when I understood that I needed to leave the business venture alone and get right with God. I needed to get back in His will for my life. Another incredible thing He showed me was all 26 chapter titles for the ABC's of this book. That alone was a good enough reason to have gone on the fast. I am so glad that I did.

I believe with every fiber of my being that God has created each and every one of us to *do*. It is our job to ask, seek, and knock. We need to find out what that means for us as individuals. I can remember earlier on in my life, I thought I would never figure out my purpose. It was so frustrating. Sometimes I failed, other times I succeeded. One thing I always did was press forward with persistency; doing what I needed to do. The more I surrendered to Him, the more I could see the vision for me.

I do not have all the answers, but I know God wants to work His power and strength through each and every one of us. I still have a long way to go, but I am learning to enjoy this journey. As we continue in this book you will get to know more about my struggles and my failures. I chose to take this narrow road instead of the broader road which I was on for many years. There are too many people on that road anyways.

What about you? Is there something that's been pressing you to do? Are you ready to do more? Are you ready to make an impact for God's Kingdom? Let's keep going. I am excited to see where God is going to take us in the next few chapters. I have no idea what our destination looks like; I'm just writing what God impresses upon me to write. At this moment, I am just as curious to see what lies ahead as you are.

MY PRAYER: Heavenly Father, You reminded me of the very first ministry I served in; serving the homeless in the streets of Atlanta. Allow me to share here in prayer with the men so they may know that You are the One who puts these type of promptings in us. When we feel Your nudge to do something outside of ourselves, we must learn that it is for a greater reason and it can be a very powerful thing if only we respond by doing. I remember as a "baby" Christian, I wanted to please You so bad. In doing so, I got involved in something that I had no idea about just because I thought it was a good way to please You. I believe Lord, that when we respond to You and do what You ask of us, You show us a different side of ourselves. Maybe it is a side that we didn't know was even there. This is where I believe change begins. So, for the men reading this prayer, I pray that we would dare to step out and *do* something and then watch what the power of God does through us.

In Jesus' name, AMEN!

CHAPTER 5
ENDURE E

"Therefore, since we are surrounded by such a huge crowd of witnesses to the life of faith, let us strip off every weight that slows us down, especially the sin that so easily trips us up. And let us run with endurance the race God has set before us." (Hebrews 12:1 NLT)

In the second verse of the scripture above (which is not shown) it tells us how we can run the race with endurance. It mentions that we do this by keeping our eyes on Jesus; the champion who initiates and perfects our faith. Because of the joy awaiting Him, He endured the cross, disregarding its shame. Now He is seated in the place of honor beside God's throne. That is great news.

Have you ever run a race? Like a 5K, 10K, 13.2, or maybe a 26.2? I'm sure some of you have. I'm sure some of you are pretty active and wisely run in preparation for upcoming races. Running requires much endurance.

There are other sports that require endurance, but for whatever reason when one speaks of endurance the first thought is usually running. I guess maybe because it's a long and tedious act.

Have you ever stopped to think about why we run? I have once before. The only answer I came up with was to stay in shape. I've run a few races in my time. But somehow, back in my running days, it went from just running to actually entering races. I guess by entering races I could get something for my efforts. What about you?

Running to me is actually very boring. It's long, drawn out, tedious, and painful. I do remember when I ran my first 13.2 and crossed the finish line and how they put that medal around my neck. And I can't forget the TLC they extended by handing me a thermal blanket at the end of a grueling 13 miles or so. After crossing the finish line and receiving the award, all the training seemed to be worth it. It was all about getting the reward. The non-runners may be wondering, "So, we run and run and run to get the reward at the end?" Yep!

The author of Hebrews likens life to running a race that requires endurance. Life is like a huge Boston Marathon. Thousands of people line up and run to receive the prize at the end of the race. Isn't this what God promises us too? Another verse in Philippians tells us to run in such a way as to get the prize.

"I press on toward the goal to win the prize for which God has called me heavenward in Christ Jesus." (Philippians 3:14)

The good news with life is that there are no medals given away for finishing the race. The prize and reward is actually to be in heaven with Jesus! That should be our goal! That beats getting a medal any day. Our training consists of everything we do, every single day. There's a lot that goes into preparing for a race. When I first started running, I had to educate myself on the art of running. The reason for this was to make sure I had the proper gear, that I was eating properly, and doing the proper stretches and exercises to minimize potential injuries. Just like in running, God has provided us with everything we need to run this race in life. We have an amazing training manual called the Bible. He has provided us with training coaches that are qualified to help train you and I for the long road ahead.

You see, this race we are in is no 5K, it's more like those ultra-running races. Those things are like 50 to 100 miles or longer. Some of them actually have the word "endurance" in their titles. Can you imagine running 100 plus miles? I have biked that long, but actually running, like with your feet, umm... I don't think so. If life is like a long ultra-marathon, how are you doing with it? There are definitely a lot of obstacles trying to keep us from finishing. Every day is a challenge; from the time you wake up until the end of the day. It can feel like you are running with a 200 lb. man on your back.

The opening verse says to "strip away every weight that slows us down".

What exactly is your 200 lbs. on your back? Porn, lust, adultery, temptation, masturbation, greed, pride, money, hobbies, anger, selfishness, low self-esteem, lack of commitment, or abuse? These are just a few heavy items we carry.

To run the race with excellence, you have got to strip away anything that is slowing you down. None of us are strong enough to keep carrying 200 lbs. on our backs. After a while we will eventually conk out. I promise you, even a 5-hour energy drink won't be enough to keep you going.

You see, there hasn't been anything created in a bottle yet to assist with endurance and perseverance, not the kind that we need anyhow. The one and only true source is God. He's running alongside each and every one of us. We only need to give Him that heavy 200 lbs. on our backs and He will do the rest. I can say with confidence that God is with you only because His Word says that He is.

"Be strong and courageous. Do not be afraid or terrified because of them, for the Lord your God goes with you; he will never leave you nor forsake you." (Deuteronomy 31:6)

In training, perseverance and endurance are usually the two words mentioned as if they are the same. Actually, both are important in this kind of race, but they aren't quite the same. Perseverance is defined as continuance till the end. And endurance is defined as using strength to continue despite pain and fatigue.

The difference between the two is that **persistence is remaining steady in hopes to finish while endurance is bearing pain so that you can finish.** Endurance is different than persistence because you have to conquer pain to endure. It is using God's strength to continue despite pain and fatigue. With God's strength you are able to continue, no matter how painful or tired you get. When I am weak He is strong. That is why it is so important as part of our training to have that relationship with God. Training as in studying His Word and much prayer. God's Word is filled with wise teachings that will help us run this race. The obstacles that we face daily should be welcomed because only out of those trials do we get stronger to overcome the next obstacle.

"Dear brothers and sisters, when troubles of any kind come your way, consider it an opportunity for great joy. For you know that when your faith is tested, your endurance has a chance to grow. So let it grow, for when your endurance is fully developed, you will be perfect and complete, needing nothing." (James 1:2-4 NLT)

I'm not saying that you should run out there and find stuff to happen to you, but you should always be aware that something could be right around the corner. I am also not saying to be fearful all the time either. Those who are diligently training have very little problem dealing with trials and temptations as they come. Why is that? Because they use their time to stay in the Word. If you find it hard to stay focused, God knows of your struggles. He knows what temptations you face each and every day. 1 Corinthians 10:13 tells us this:

"No temptation has overtaken you except what is common to mankind. And God is faithful; he will not let you be tempted beyond what you can bear. But when you are tempted, he will also provide a way out so that you can endure it."

You see that? You are not alone with your temptations and distractions. This verse says "No temptation has overtaken you except what is common to man." Your struggles are not new; not to God anyway. Now, you may be tempted by something different than the next guy, but don't you worry. Whatever it is, it has already been dealt with by someone somewhere in the past.

The individuals that are able to stay focused on God are the men who stay in prayer daily. They stay strong in the things of God. They don't let worldly things interfere with their training. They focus on the things above and not things on earth. These are the type of men that God can use. Men like Paul, look at what he wrote here:

"However, I consider my life worth nothing to me; my only aim is to finish the race and complete the task the Lord Jesus has given me--the task of testifying to the good news of God's grace." (Acts 20:24)

Paul knew exactly what he needed to do. There wasn't any question. He lived for God, that's it. No confusion whether he should do this or that. He simply did that which he was created for. He endured all kinds of persecutions for the sake of sharing Jesus.

When I left home at age 17 due to all the physical and emotional abuse, I recall not having a plan about anything. I didn't know where I was going, what I going to do, where I was going to get my next meal, or where I was going to lay my head. I left with knowing nothing. I wasn't sure which was worse, the physical beatings or the emotional beatings. Perhaps it was the beating from life that I ended up getting. I guess I really didn't think the whole "leaving" thing through properly.

Oh well, once I left it was too late. My pride wouldn't let me go back even if I wanted to. I couldn't. Something inside of me never even thought about going back. I was going to take on whatever came my way and this decision is what began my first lesson in endurance.

During this time, I latched on to a fictional character by the name of Rocky Balboa. I know, bad acting and all that, but it wasn't about the movie so much as it was about the story line. The fact that he would get knocked down and then get back up every time was mind blowing. I've been knocked down a whole lot, and I've always gotten right back up too. Sometimes it took a little bit longer to get up, but I got back up. That's what our race is about. God knows our weaknesses and He knows that we will get knocked down. It's about getting up and continuing to move forward. This is one of my all-time favorite quotes:

"Let me tell you something you already know. The world ain't all sunshine and rainbows. It's a very mean and nasty place. And I don't care how tough you are, it will beat you to your knees and keep you there permanently if you let it. You, me, or nobody is gonna hit as hard as life. But it ain't about how hard ya hit. It's about how hard you can get hit and keep moving forward. How much you can take and keep moving forward. That's how winning is done!"

— Sylvester Stallone, *Rocky Balboa*

I am so grateful to God because I know that even when I did not know Him, He was always right there. It's only because of Him that I am still alive. During those years when I thought I was all alone trying to survive by sleeping in abandoned cars, train station bathrooms, breaking into basement cellars or in storage rooms, God gave me the spirit of endurance and perseverance to arrive humbled many years later. The moment I learned about God and His grace towards me, all the years of pain, hurt, abandonment, and anger now seem somehow worth it. He literally kept me alive while I walked through the valley of the shadow of death, more than once. He loved me so much that He sustained me until I surrendered my life over to Him at the age of 36. I know now that

I can run one of those ultra-marathons because God is with me. What is your story?

If you are reading this book, then it means you are alive. If you are alive and still running the race of life, it is because God is with you. He loves you so much that He is going to keep you until you surrender yourself to Him. He will then open your eyes and be able to show you His plans for your life. I know for a fact that God's plans are way better than any plan you or I could come up with. It's not about how hard you hit, it's about how hard you can *get* hit and keep moving forward! Stop trying to hit back, you are only tiring yourself out. Let God do some of the hitting now. I promise you, He can do it much better than we can. Focus on this race. I don't know about you, but I'm going to finish this race for the prize. I pray that I see you at the finish line. Let's celebrate together!

MY PRAYER:

Heavenly Father, HELP! Yes, that is what is shouted out during hard and difficult times. I pray that more men would shout out that word "HELP" to You when things are hard and seem impossible to do. I believe, with You all things are possible, and You can get us through anything. I pray that men would learn to not give up, but to really know and understand what it means to get endurance from You to keep going. Endurance requires humility, not pride. So I pray that we would put away our stubbornness and prideful ways and reach out to You for help in running the race that is set before us.

In Jesus' name, AMEN!

CHAPTER 6

FAITH

"Now faith is the substance of things hoped for, the evidence of things not seen." (Hebrews 11:1)

I'll tell you what faith is... faith is me writing this book. Faith is not putting confidence in my capabilities, because I already tried to do that and failed. Faith is however me putting confidence in God's capabilities especially with writing this book and believing that He will guide me as I type the words. Furthermore, that He will provide the means and avenues to get this book where He wants it to go. This is one of those "stepping out in faith" assignments.

Scripture tell us in James 1:17, "In the same way, faith by itself, if it is not accompanied by action, is dead". Faith without works is dead. What good is it to say you have faith, if you don't put some activity behind it, right? In chapter 2, we learned about believing in something bigger than our self. That's kind of like faith, except I believe faith goes a bit deeper. Faith is a foundational component that we all need.

God created us to have faith. You have faith whether you know it or not. If you don't think it takes faith to stick a key in a keyhole and turn it so that it causes electrical currents and all other combustions to take place, you're loco. Then you have to drive this thing along roads and highways, in and out of traffic, while all along you are relying on parts to work. That takes faith.

I believe there are so many other things that God wants us to pay more attention to when it comes to this word. Like we talked about in the last chapter, when obstacles get in the way of our everyday life, we somehow still get through them. God wants us to acknowledge Him as the one who got us through it. That's faith; well, it's a start anyway. Truth be told - faith is still more than that.

Let me give you another way to look at what faith is. Faith is belief with strong conviction; firm belief in something for which there may be no tangible proof; complete trust in or devotion to. Faith is the opposite of doubt. Faith is possibly the single-most important element of the Christian life. Hebrews 11:6 states:

"And without faith it is impossible to please God, because anyone who comes to him must believe that he exists and that he rewards those

who earnestly seek him."

Here's why I said that faith was a bit more than just acknowledging God. Scripture explains that the source of faith is God:

"For it is by grace you have been saved, through faith--and this not from yourselves, it is the gift of God--not by works, so that no one can boast."
(Ephesians 2:8, 9)

While writing on the the 3rd day of my fast, I eagerly anticipated what God was going to have me write. I had searched the internet for some clever things to write and even tried to grab a sentence or two from here and there, but I didn't find anything. I believe that God is telling me to trust Him. Just like with the other chapters prior to this one, He had been working, so why would He stop now?

Guys, as you read this you can believe that I am putting my faith to work. I have to. I am searching and waiting for Him to give me the words to write. I am not a writer, nor do I have any idea as to what to write. Remember, I have tried this on my own a few times and failed. When you set out to do what seems to be "the impossible", that's when God's power and strength can shine through. When you set out to do what God asks of you, especially when you don't know how, that's where faith in God steps in! Your spirit man says, "Yes, I can!"

To step out into the wet, cold, and unknown world requires faith. Focusing on Him strengthens our faith, while lacking focus weakens our faith. If we look at the passage in the Bible that tells of Jesus walking on the water and Peter doing the same, you can see where this statement is true.

"Then Peter got down out of the boat, walked on the water and came toward Jesus. But when he saw the wind, he was afraid and began to sink. He then cried out, "Lord, save me!" Immediately Jesus reached out his hand and caught him. "You of little faith," Jesus said. "Why did you doubt?" (Matthew 14:29-31)

I would call this "shaky or wavering" faith. We see that when Peter took his focus off of Jesus, who is our source of faith, and put it on the storm, he sank. Don't we do that very same thing? Everything I am writing about requires our utmost attention towards Him. Our focus has to be on Him, and not on the storms in life. Hebrews 11:6 plainly says, "Without faith, it is impossible to please God."

I just remembered something that happened to me a long time ago concerning faith. This had to have happened sometime in the late 90's or so. It was my first test of faith. I was running a sprinkler system company around this time, and my first wife and I with our two kids were living in a townhouse in Alpharetta, Georgia. Now, Alpharetta was and still is an upscale and affluent area. It was expensive to live there, but we just *had* to live there.

Back then it was the thing to tell people that you had an Alpharetta address when they asked where you live. Stupid, I know. That was a long time ago. Anyway, business was not going too well at this particular time and I found myself falling into a mild depression. We got behind on our rent because I hadn't had any work for a few weeks now. No Installations equals no money to pay bills. I remember on this particular day lying on the couch half asleep, clicking through the channels and this loud woman was on the air talking about faith, particularly having faith in God. The way she talked about it caught my attention so I sat up and watched her. Can you guess who that loud woman was? Yeah it was Joyce Meyer. She wasn't loud with her tone loud, but her personality and her message was loud.

Anyways, it got my attention. I listened with such an interest. I remember feeling something rise in me, something that felt good. I no longer was feeling sorry for myself or worrying about the rent. I felt a calm spirit. She talked about how trusting God and having faith produces great things. She said how God wants the best for each of us and how all we have to do is to step out and believe. I watched her complete program. I felt pretty good for a little while, until my wife came home and asked if I received any calls today. She was upset and worried about us paying the rent. I tried to share with her what I had watched earlier in the day about having faith in God and how He will take care of us. She wasn't having any of it.

Later that night after dinner, I was washing the dishes and thinking about everything Joyce had talked about. In front of the sink was a window with bushes nearly the same height. As I was washing the dishes I was looking out the window and just basking in all that Joyce had talked about when all of a sudden I noticed something crumpled up on one of the bushes. I knew what I thought it was, so I ran outside and grabbed it, opened it up and it was a miracle! I ran over to my wife at that time and waved this wrinkled $100.00 bill in her face and shouted, "See, I told you that God is going to take care of us if we have some faith!" She just replied back, "That's only a hundred dollars. We need a few more of those."

I wasn't going to let her steal my joy. Yeah, I know that it was only $100.00, but I believed God was trying to tell me that anything was possible. He was going to take care of us. I just believed it deep inside me. A few days had passed and we were down to two days or so to come up with $1,500.00. After finding the $100 bill, I kept watching Joyce Meyer, believing that God was going to do a miracle. My phone hadn't rang for about 5 weeks and I remember calling someone to make sure that it worked. I was getting a little antsy, but still believed and I remembered telling myself that I have got to have faith. That's all I would say at that point.

I believe it was around 4:30 pm on a Friday and we had to have rent paid by Tuesday or something, when my phone rang. I almost missed the call because I didn't comprehend that my phone was ringing. It was like I had forgotten what a ringing phone sounded like. It was the neighbor of a customer who I had installed a 4-zone sprinkler system for. She wanted me to give her an estimate. If she said yes it would mean a deposit on the work to be done which would be enough to buy the materials necessary and pay the rent. Can you believe that I got the job and she paid the deposit? I was able to pay rent!

Before I paid the rent though I took the cash, which was all in hundreds and fanned them in front of my wife's face. I shouted again, "See what faith can do!" All she did was smile and took the money out of my hands. I was beyond ecstatic. My first encounter with faith and God showed up big time!

Needless to say, this didn't last long as I continued living life the way I wanted. It was like I had forgotten what God can do and what He did. It wouldn't be until many years later that He would finally get a hold of me.

I have so many faith stories. There are so many times that God came through. As my walk with Christ grew, so did my faith in Him. I have seen Him do some amazing miracles, not just in my life or my family's life, but also in the life of others. Having faith and exercising it can be so powerful. Having faith in Him can even bring back the dead! You can't just say that you have faith; you actually have to *move* in faith to activate it.

I have learned through the years that faith isn't a button that you turn on when you need it and off when you don't. Faith is on-going; everyday, all the time, in good and in bad times. God wants to use us in ways that we can't imagine, but as men, we have got to get to that place where faith is second nature. I mean to the point where you can leave it in His hands and He will see it through.

I mentioned a little earlier in this chapter that the opposite of faith is doubt. You either have faith or you doubt. Where are you today with your faith? What has God done in your life where you needed to have faith in Him? Have you been like me, forgetting what God can do by trying to do things here and there in your own ability? I hope not. Because I'm here to tell you today that God wants to show you so much more. You will be able to do *so* much more in your life if you just step out in faith!

What do you desire to do, but are too afraid to do it? Joyce calls it "stinkin' thinkin'". Don't let Satan take away what God has for you. You can even close your eyes if you want to and just step out and imagine God catching you. All it takes is faith the size of a mustard seed. Look at what Jesus said:

"Because you have so little faith, truly I tell you, if you have faith as small as a mustard seed, you can say to this mountain, 'Move from here to there,' and it will move. Nothing will be impossible for you."

(Matthew 17:20)

Granted Jesus speaks in parables, but what He is telling us in reality is that it doesn't take much faith for God to work. It takes true authentic faith for God to do the impossible where you thought it was impossible. I believe that God is going to do amazing things with this book. I know that God wants to reach you, yeah you. He sees you right this moment reading this very sentence. He is waiting for you to just simply ask Him to help you right now. He wants to help you step out in faith with that thing in your heart.

You see, God put a desire in your heart. All you have to do is believe and have faith that He will guide you in that endeavor. You already have confirmation. You already know that you are supposed to do it. What? I'm sorry... What? You are waiting... Oh, well let me cut you off for a quick second then. You don't need to wait for any better time. That is your fear talking. You don't need to wait until this or that. Let God sort those things out. I know this chapter is speaking to someone directly, because as I am writing, I can see that God has been trying to get your attention; especially on this topic.

God is impressing upon me to tell you to stop. Literally, stop right now, wherever you are and whatever you are doing. Even stop reading this. Stop and just begin to pray. I am going to stop typing right now and pray as well.

MY PRAYER: Dear Lord, I ask You in Your Son's name that

You would touch each and every man or individual who has gotten to this point in the book. Give them the courage to receive from You, Lord. Their faith is right in front of them to grab a hold of and activate. Encourage them to step out into that which You have already impressed upon them to do. Take away any fear, doubt, or even pride that might be hindering them to walk confidently in their faith in You. God, I believe this book is from You. You have been the guide to my writing process, so I pray blessings over every person who reads what You wanted me to write. May each person also know that this act has been done out of faith and obedience to You. Father to those men that are hesitant to move forward, I pray that Your words would ease them and reassure them that your promises are truth. You are with each and every one of us as we run this race. You know all of our struggles and obstacles that we have faced and will yet still face. I pray Lord that we will move forward into what You have for us. May we have faith in knowing that You have our best interest at heart. As long as we continue to exercise our faith, we will be able to grow in You and with You. You, God, are our victory!

I pray this in the name of Jesus, AMEN!

CHAPTER 7

GIVE

"Give generously to them and do so without a grudging heart; then because of this, the Lord your God will bless you in all your work and in everything you put your hand to." (Deuteronomy 15:10)

For some of you, I'm sure this is a chapter title that makes you cringe. Actually, I'm sure a lot of these titles in this book may make you cringe. They are all very important though. Giving is a very important topic, but don't worry, I'm not merely talking about opening up your wallet. Although opening up your wallet to give some of your hard earned cash is important, there are other things that we need to give which we'll discuss in this chapter as well.

Where are you though with giving? I mean what is your take on the matter? Is this a weak area in your life? I know for a lot of people it is. For me it was. I can remember when we started tithing at our church in Norcross. Back then, Carrie and I weren't making much money and it took a whole lot for us to tithe 10%. At first I only did it out of obedience. But giving is so much more than just the tithing or about money. I began seeing that revelation when Carrie and I got involved with the homeless ministry at Victory World Church.

That ministry was under the umbrella of the Mercy Team ministry and they partnered up with another ministry called 7 Bridges to Recovery headed by Pastor Dan Wells or Pastor Seven as everyone called him. I tell you, this was an amazing experience. Pastor Seven has an amazing testimony which I won't go into detail here, but he basically got out of prison and with the little money he had, he would walk around the inner city of Atlanta and help the homeless. He sometimes slept under the bridges with them and he ministered to them, sharing his testimony about how God changed his life while in prison. He was a pretty hardcore guy; I believe he would have been considered an O.G. – (original gangsta) in prison.

What attracted me to him and what he was doing was the similarities that he and I shared. I was able to see this tough guy love on people. I never saw such a thing before. Within a short time, Carrie and I were going multiple days in the week to serve outside of the church's ministry going. I was floored at how giving time and sharing moments with the homeless made me feel. Like I said, we didn't have bunches of money to give, but what I learned was loving people is also giving.

While I was spending time and listening to their stories, I was giving. Carrie and I got so involved that we actually left our church for a while to help Pastor Seven and his team full time. I believe the time spent with 7 Bridges taught me so much about giving, and that was all I wanted to do.

We ended up back at Victory and the giving continued when Carrie and I were chosen to lead and help start a ministry called Celebrate Recovery. Celebrate Recovery is a Christian 12 Step Program started by John Baker from Rick Warren's Saddleback Church. In this ministry all you can do is give, because those who participate are in such dire need. Unless one is prepared to give much, this ministry is not for them. I can tell you this though, the more I gave, the more I got. You give little, you get little in return. You give much, you get much in return. It's that simple. Remember this verse:

"Whoever sows sparingly will also reap sparingly, and whoever sows generously will also reap generously." (2 Corinthians 9:6)

Here's the thing about giving; you never really know how it feels to give until you give. I only got involved in ministry because Pastor Dennis from Victory World Church taught men to step up and serve. So, I needed to figure out what to do. I served at the church on the security team, but I wanted to give more. That's the reason I got involved in the Mercy Team and found the homeless ministry. From there I just felt the need to keep giving whatever I could. Not only did we tithe appropriately, but we gave above our tithe. We just felt the *need* to give.

For those of you that might not know this, **giving is one of the most satisfying acts one can do.** I share my giving activities only to express to you how important it is in your walk with Christ. I believe that giving is a Christian's duty. We need to be intentional at finding where to give. Jesus was all about giving and God loves a cheerful giver.

"Each of you should give what you have decided in your heart to give, not reluctantly or under compulsion, for God loves a cheerful giver."

(2 Corinthians 9:7)

So, as you see, according to this scripture you should give what your heart leads you to. Giving isn't about giving money necessarily, as I mentioned before. What I believe the take away from this chapter is the fact that giving is a gift that God has given us. How is it a gift, you may ask? It's a gift because we get to give whatever it is away. Giving is such a gratifying experience for our inner man, our spirit.

I believe God designed it that way on purpose. Nowadays, I intentionally try and find opportunities where I can give. I suggest you try it too. If you aren't a giver, I challenge you to step out in faith and just give. Did you know when you participate in a men's group or a small group, you are giving. Yes, initially you sign up for yourself to be part of a group of men, but in reality each participant is there to give; not just their time, but their experiences to one another.

As you may know, there are many benefits in giving. By giving of our self to others, it is how some healings are received. Giving is a form of worship to God and probably the most important reason why we should give. This is a great benefit to you because God blesses you in return. In the verse you read at the beginning of this chapter out of Deuteronomy it says that exact thing. It said: "Give generously to them and do so without a grudging heart; then because of this, the Lord your God will bless you in all your work and in everything you put your hand to."

Yes, this was directed at the Israelites, but just like so many other verses in the Bible, this one applies to us as well. Within the discussion of giving is the word tithing. As if giving wasn't hard enough for some of you, we must tithe too. Tithing is giving, but I see it as more of a "must do". Some of you reading this might not agree, and that's your choice. I believe serving God includes everything that is in His Word. But if serving the Lord seems undesirable to you, then choose for yourselves this day who you will serve, whether it is the gods of your ancestors or the gods of the land you are living in. But as for me and my house, we will serve the Lord. I mention the passage of scripture here again to emphasize the importance of following and being obedient to *all* of God's Word; the New Testament and the Old Testament. I refer guys to the following verse whenever the topic of tithing arises:

"Bring the whole tithe into the storehouse that there may be food in my house. Test me in this," says the Lord Almighty, "and see if I will not throw open the floodgates of heaven and pour out so much blessing that there will not be room enough to store it."
(Malachi 3:10)

I believe the rewards of giving and tithing outweigh the rewards of not doing so. Either I have faith in God and His Word or I don't. It is not wise to pick and choose which part of the Bible we are going to follow. It's all or nothing.

The next time you are in a debate with yourself about whether or not you should give or tithe or even how much, don't answer it on your own, but lay it before God and see what He has to say about it. If you're wondering why we have to give 10% for our tithes, here's the short answer: **Tithing was created for our benefit.** It is to teach us how to keep God first in our lives and how to be unselfish people. Unselfish people make better husbands, wives, friends, relatives, employees and employers. God has our best interest at heart and is only teaching us how to prosper over time. He knew from the beginning that we would have problems with money. The love for money is the root of all evil, so

He made a way for His people to not get so attached to it, and that is done by us giving the first 10% of what we earn back to Him. By putting God first, we have to consistently rely on Him and that's a good thing.

MY PRAYER:

Heavenly Father, for men, giving seems to be something that is getting harder and harder to do. I pray that we would have a heart that never stops giving. I pray that we would give You our time and our full tithe as a priority. I ask that You would help men to step up at home, in church, and even in the community and just give whatever You put in their minds and hearts to give. Giving is serving someone else, so I pray that men would put their wants and desires aside and seek out the needs of others. Lord, to be like Christ is to give, may we all live our lives accordingly. Thank You, Father.

In Jesus' name I pray, AMEN!

CHAPTER 8
HUMBLE H

"If my people, who are called by my name, will humble themselves and pray and seek my face and turn from their wicked ways, then I will hear from heaven, and I will forgive their sin and will heal their land."

(2 Chronicles 7:14)

Humility is something that is gained and practiced as we grow in wisdom and grace. Easton's 1897 Bible Dictionary defines humility as: a prominent Christian grace. It is a state of mind well pleasing to God; it preserves the soul in tranquility and makes us patient under trials.

Biblically speaking, humility is the opposite of pride. How many of you reading this have reached the highest level of humility that is humanly possible? Be careful. I wouldn't answer this if I were you. This is one of those questions that you just can't answer. If you are a humble man, then you should already know that.

So, I'll go first and say that I still have some work to be done. I actually have work to do on every single topic of this book. I believe this is one of the hardest things to be, especially in today's society. There are numerous career positions that require much more from you than being humble. Although, some of the most successful men have actually been labeled as some very humble men. As men, if we could really get this down and just submit ourselves to God's Lordship, He will change us into the humble men that He desires us to be. Our impact for the Kingdom would be limitless in this world.

So many of us just won't give up the pride though. We feel the need to hold on to some of our old traits. The more humble we are, the more God can trust us. A completely submitted heart is what God is looking for; anything less than that is just not good enough. I wrote in the opening of this chapter one of the definitions:

Humility is a state of mind well pleasing to God.

"Humble yourselves, therefore, under God's mighty hand, that he may lift you up in due time." (1 Peter 5:6)

This scripture really strikes home. You see, I have been praying and waiting for God to lift me up; not just lift me, but the MAN ON PURPOSE ministry as well. I couldn't figure out why God would impress upon me to begin this ministry only to have it slowly fizzle away. I guess it was not until recently when I discovered why. All of these traits that I am writing about in this book are very important, but I believe humility is very high at the top of importance. You and I can't really fulfill anything the way God wants us to without being humble about it. Humility is a foundational trait that shows others that Christ lives within us.

I realize that I need to be honest with myself and God that there are still pride issues hindering me from receive everything He is trying to do with MAN ON PURPOSE. Since I began dealing with my pride issues, God has released me to write this book. Just like we discussed in the first chapter about men and their pride, I'm not completely "pride-less". What I am saying is that my prideful ways have significantly decreased and I am conscious of it. It's that way because I pray about it every day and ask God to keep me humble.

Carrie helps me with my pride quite often. She makes me aware when I say something that is prideful. A lot of the time, us guys say something and we don't even see it as being prideful, but others do. That is why it is so important to give your wife and/or accountability partner the freedom to speak into your life. I've also learned not to argue about if the words I said were prideful or not, and what I meant or didn't mean. I now just accept it as being prideful and later lift it to God in prayer. He has definitely let me know, and He will do the same for you.

Prayer in itself shows growth, maturity, and humility. I never said that being humble means to be some kind of "door mat" or "push over". By no means. What I am saying is that it shows much more maturity when we receive correction and ask God to show us when we don't see it our self. If you try and defend yourself against your wife, it's just going to end up ugly. A humble man listens to reason and makes the necessary adjustments. Your wife is not the enemy. She's the one that makes you look good. She's the one that wants the best for you, that's why she corrects you. She's not out to harm you or out to get you. If you thought that about your wife, then maybe you should not have married her to begin with. But since you did marry her, remember, God intended your spouse to be your rib, your helpmate; so let her help, mate.

I have learned a few things about who I am today, and one of them is this: I would not be half the man I am without this amazing woman that God has given me. It hasn't been easy, but because she truly loves me, I have changed so much. Of course, God did the changing, nevertheless it had to start with an obedient and humble heart. We will discuss obedience in chapter 15, but I believe humility comes out of obedience. Remember the statement I opened this chapter with: Humility is something that is gained and practiced as we grow in wisdom and grace. Wisdom, my friends, teaches you to be obedient which in turn can humble you over time. No, it does not happen overnight, but it does happen.

Humility is all about others, whereas pride is all about you. Be honest and ask yourself: Do you put the interests of others before your own or are you a self-seeking? Being a strong man in God's eyes means that you are a humble man; because it takes strength to be humble. For most of us, we have been taught that being a strong man means the opposite of being humble. Why do you think we need God to help us? Because when we are weak, He is strong. We have to rely on Him for humility. You and I are not capable of humility on our own. Look at this verse in James:

"But he gives us more grace. That is why Scripture says: "God opposes the proud but shows favor to the humble." (James 4:6)

It is God's grace that He gives us humility. Humility allows us to "turn the other cheek" so to speak. What I mean is this: it's easy to fly off the handle and go off on your wife, kids, coworker, or whomever. What's *hard* is to repress the pride and stay quiet and just agree with that person. A humble man can do that. A humble man is wise and understands that flying off the handle does not benefit anyone or anything. So, for the sake of peace, a humble man can take a hit or two and keep it moving. A humble man sees the bigger picture, where a prideful man is more interested in momentary satisfaction regardless of the consequences.

You see, a humble man doesn't have to be right, even though he might be 100% right about an issue. The point of humility does not have to prove that you are right. A humble man can say something like, "Oh really?" Because he knows that causing a riff is not worth the possibility of an argument. I'm not saying that you have to just agree with everyone about everything all the time. I'm saying that a humble man knows when and with whom he can challenge something. Not everyone is mature enough to be told something against their will or beliefs. How do I know?

Because knowing comes with wisdom! This is another topic that we will discuss later on in the book.

I have learned that wisdom is the "Grand-daddy" of all traits to have. Why do you think Solomon asked to receive it when God questioned him? He knew the value of wisdom. Wisdom controls the decisions you make. So, wisdom tells us that humility wins each and every time. It might not look that way right at that moment, but trust me it does. Humility wins every time.

As with each and every one of these topics, take a look in the mirror and pray about them. See what God would impress upon you about what to work on next. It starts with coming to God in a state of humility to receive his compassionate rebuke. This is the true and only way to change the "you" that has been created by your influences, environment and choices.

MY PRAYER: Heavenly Father, You, Lord, are our Creator. You

know us better than anyone else in this world. I come before You with a humble heart seeking Your wisdom and truth. Lord, I ask that You show us the ugliness that's inside of us; the parts that You did not put there. We are the one that have put these parts in us by living and doing how we wanted. God, we understand now that those parts are nothing more than selfishness and pride. I want to surrender my life to You so that You can begin the change process in me. We can only do this with a humble heart. Today I ask You, Father, help us where we are. Help us to become more humble day after day. We want our lives to be a testimony of Your glorious power and walk in the purpose that you have for us. I thank You so much, Lord.

In Jesus name I pray, AMEN!

CHAPTER 9
INTENTIONAL I

"Be diligent in these matters; give yourself wholly to them, so that everyone may see your progress. Watch your life and doctrine closely. Persevere in them, because if you do, you will save both yourself and your hearers." (1 Timothy 4:15, 16)

In chapter 4 we discussed "DO" which is very similar to being intentional, however I believe there is a slight difference. Doing is the result of being "INTENTIONAL". You see, being intentional means that you set out on purpose "to do" something. That means being intentional about something comes first before the act of something. Again, doing is the completion of being intentional. Make sense? Do you get it? This topic is one of my favorites to talk about. This word is what started Man On Purpose; well not the actual word itself, but a teaching on it from my leadership mentor, John Maxwell.

In February 2012, I had the opportunity to get a John Maxwell Leadership certification in West Palm Beach, Florida. It was the second class of many more that have taken place over the last few years. On the last day of the class, John Maxwell himself appeared before us and introduced us to his brand new, nearly published book. It was so raw that the actual title hadn't been finalized yet. The book was still going through editing. He did have the titles to each chapter, nevertheless, and that was what he shared with us.

The very first chapter caught my attention: "The Law of Intentionality". In this chapter, John explains how growth just doesn't happen. He then asked the question, "Do you have a plan for growth? Everything in this book or in any other book won't and can't grow you unless you are intentional about getting intentional and then coming up with a plan to act on."

Being intentional is all about putting forth the effort required to grow yourself in this journey. I am not the same angry, bad attitude, feeling-sorry-for-myself, selfish, prideful, hurt, lustful guy I was in 2002 when I met Carrie, my wife of 9 years now. I'm not going to pretend like I had some fabulous plan to change and grow to become a better person. Actually it was just the opposite. I had zero plans, and zero idea of what I was doing. The only thing I had going for me was determination.

It wasn't until 2005 when intentional life change began for me. I mentioned before about going to church for the first time, and shortly after receiving Jesus as my Lord and Savior. Even after committing my life to Him, all I knew to do was just hang on for the ride. I had to be intentional in allowing God to do whatever He wanted to do to get me to the destination; which, by the way I haven't reached yet. None of us have gotten there yet. Not the final destination anyway.

I mentioned a few sentences back that the word intentional is what helped launch Man On Purpose, so let me further explain. After attending the 3-day John Maxwell certification course, I returned home motivated and ready to change lives by teaching leadership; John Maxwell Leadership. I invested my time by putting together mastermind groups and teaching on a few different books written by the leadership guru.

It wasn't until Saturday morning April 18, 2012 that I began receiving these impressions from God about being who He has called me to be on purpose, being intentional; something about ministry. Then it all became clear. I was supposed to put together a men's ministry and I was to call it Man On Purpose with the tagline: Become the man you are intended to be with purpose, on purpose. A men's event was written in the details and I was to talk about the book John Maxwell had not yet published: *The 15 Invaluable Laws of Growth*. I had permission to speak on this topic with the skeleton that he gave to our group at the leadership certification in February. I was excited, but also not sure how it all was supposed to happen. I had been out of work since 2010 and unemployment had run out. Teaching mastermind groups was not happening the way I had hoped, but I continued to press forward.

I remember thinking that God had finally revealed my purpose to me. I knew it wasn't going to be easy, but nothing worthwhile ever is, right? I remember also thinking how huge these shoes were to fill, but God quickly corrected me by telling me not to focus on the size of the giant, but focus only on Him and this vision will happen. He also impressed upon me to be intentional with everything I do. It was very important to be intentional. The whole foundation of Man On Purpose isn't that I have arrived and that I have all the answers; no not at all. The foundation of Man On Purpose is for me and for you to be intentional with our walk with Jesus. He knows that we will slip up, but it's about what's in our heart that matter most.

Are you a man to give up and give in easily? Or are you a man that messes up, but keeps moving forward and stays pressing into God, intentionally? Does your heart say to be purposeful with everything you do concerning Him? One of the things I feel God has put on my heart to share is the fact that so many men are intentional with "things" other than godly things. These things have absolutely nothing to do with serving others or growing God's kingdom. These other things show that we are intentional in serving our self when this happens. I believe the priorities are off kilter, and then we wonder why things are not working out at home. Pursuing other things do not fix what is happening with our walk with God and it surely doesn't fix our relationship with our wife and kids.

Being intentional about doing something about these issues however does fix our relationships. I believe the most intentional thing I ever said and done was actually following through and taking my family to church. I was so intentional. I said, "That's it! We are going to *@%$!%& church tomorrow morning!!!" The crazy part is that we actually went and I haven't stopped going since!

Nothing happens out of doing nothing. You have got to be intentional with your direction. You have got to ask God for direction and guidance. Part of being intentional requires you to put your foot down and make hard and sometimes risky decisions. I believe so very strongly that when you stand up and do the things that are necessary for your personal growth, for your Jesus growth, and for your family growth, God will make a way for you to do so. You have to make the first move though, that's where being intentional comes in.

Here's the deal guys, all I'm trying to do is share a simple fact with you. In order to walk in your complete purpose, you have got to be intentional in finding out how to do it. Each of us has a part to play in whether we fulfill our calling and purpose or not. Doing nothing brings about no results whatsoever. Therefore, doing something brings about, well, the results that God has in store for you. You will never be a "complete" man until you are being intentional with your purpose.

It's funny how we tell our kids, "Before you can go out and play, make sure to do your chores and homework first." We teach our kids to follow the priorities set for them, yet we as men don't even follow the priorities set by our Father in heaven, God.

Your kids must see you following God's priorities before they will ever freely follow yours on their own. As the man, if you are not serious about being intentional with your own growth, how can you expect that from anyone else? I think back to my own Christian walk when I was still struggling with all kinds of issues. I could only realistically expect the same results out of others that I was portraying myself. If they saw that I was being intentional with my growth with God and practicing what I was learning, I'm sure they would respond to that in a positive way. John Maxwell teaches this in another one of his books, *The 21 Irrefutable Laws of Leadership*.

This particular law is entitled: The Law of the Lid – Leadership Ability Determines a Person's Level of Effectiveness. This basically means our level of leadership can only take us as far as those we lead. Until you raise your lid to a higher leadership level, you will only be as effective as your current level. This is the same across the board. In order to be effective you have got to be intentional in raising that lid. How do you do that? It helps that you are reading this book, but there are so many other great resources that will grow your inner being to the level that can affect all avenues of your life.

Like I said before, you have to ask God for direction and guidance. I have been able to use everything I intentionally went after as well as things I had zero control over as a learning experience. It has become a means of gaining wisdom throughout the years and I have put it to good use for God's kingdom. I have done so by empowering men to become the men they are intended to be, with purpose, on purpose.

For me, if I had not learned to be intentional, I would have never written this book or started Man On Purpose. All I know is this: God will show us what to do when we are intentionally doing what He desires. I continue to be intentional about growing into the best man I can be and becoming the man that He intended for me to be.

There is a promise that holds true for me and every one of you. Therefore, I will leave you with this verse. It is one that has really gotten my attention over the last couple of years and has helped me to be more intentional.

"For I know the plans I have for you," declares the Lord, "plans to prosper you and not to harm you, plans to give you hope and a future." (Jeremiah 29:11)

Oh, by the way, this was the very first scripture that I memorized when I became a Christian, simply because of what I mentioned above.

MY PRAYER:

Heavenly Father, I know that a lot of men struggle with being intentional. Lord, I pray that we men would not focus on the pain, the discomfort, or what we can't do or what we don't have. I pray we focus solely on what You tell us. I desire that men will be intentional with finding their purpose so that their lives may be filled with everything You have in store for them. Lord, I believe the more we step out in faith to do something, the more You will reveal to us. This ultimately leads us into our purpose, the specific one You have for us. In order to find our purpose, we must be intentional in all that we do for You. I believe, the more intentional we are, the more You can work in us, through us, and for us. Therefore, I ask for Your help, Lord. Show us, lead us, and guide us.

In Jesus' name, AMEN!

CHAPTER 10

JOY

10

J

"Rejoice in the Lord always. I will say it again: Rejoice! Let your gentleness be evident to all. The Lord is near." (Philippians 4:4, 5)

Well, this is a topic that you don't hear much of during men's events or any other kind of men's gatherings, for that matter. I believe there are a lot of men out there who really don't know or understand this "foreign" word. On the other hand, I know men everywhere know about the word "happiness". Happiness is frequently used by Christians and non-Christians alike. Happiness has been taught as the "thing" to go after in your life. Movies such as Will Smith's hit film, "The Pursuit of Happyness" focuses on the word, and it's even in our Declaration of Independence.

But here's the thing. The happiness that the world offers is a very weak imitation of the true joyfulness that God can give us. In my experiences, I have come to find that happiness and joyfulness are not the same thing.

I believe what God gives is joy and that is what we should be chasing after, not the temporary feeling of happiness.

Let me explain what I believe to be the differences between the two. Joy is a deep, spiritual fulfillment that allows you to rejoice, worship, and praise God no matter the circumstances. The situation, whether good or bad, doesn't matter when it comes to joy. The focus stays on God. When things are good, we give God praise, and when things are bad, we give God praise. Happiness, however, is a sense of satisfaction that comes and goes as the circumstances change. It goes along with a mood or a feeling that one experiences. When everything is going good, there is happiness. When one thing goes bad, happiness jumps out of the window.

"The good times of the wicked are short-lived; godless joy is only momentary." (Job 20:5 MSG)

There can be no true joy apart from God.

As this statement applies, there cannot be true joy without God because He is the source of joy. As the world is running around pursuing happiness, there is something much greater that we can have and all it takes is a relationship with God, our Creator. Why wouldn't I want something that is more satisfying and fulfilling? Happiness will only be what it is, momentary satisfaction. A joyful person can still have moments of unhappiness and be completely fine. Do you think that a joyful person won't get upset about something? Isn't Jesus the example of joy? The Scriptures say in Matthew 21:12, 13:

"And Jesus entered the temple and drove out all those who were buying and selling in the temple, and overturned the tables of the moneychangers and the seats of those who were selling doves. And He said to them, "It is written, 'My house shall be called a house of prayer'; but you are making it a robbers' den."

This scripture shows us that Jesus was upset about this situation, but He didn't lose his joy in the process. Like I said before, happiness comes and goes. There isn't anything wrong with happiness, but why settle when there is something much deeper and more gratifying for your soul? This is a special something that truly shows who God is and it literally connects us to Him. Joy is the word!

So many people have sought happiness through entertainment or a certain performer they just "love". Some seek happiness in athletic endeavors, hobbies, traveling, dancing, fashion, home improvements, wealth, status, lust, alcohol, food, or drugs. Except for a brief period of satisfaction and sense of well-being, these all fail. That's what happiness is. Look at the last sentence again: Except for a brief period of satisfaction and a *sense* of well-being, these all fail.

What happens when these things are gone? When you have no more money? When you've lost your job? When you can no longer catch, throw or shoot the ball the way you used to? What happens to the people who run after these things for their source of happiness? They become the exact opposite of happy... miserable. Then after becoming miserable they must chase after what made them happy from the beginning again. Unfortunately, when they can't find that "something" that makes them truly happy, they numb their pain because they are no longer happy. It's a downward cycle. This means your focus has become sex, drugs, alcohol, or working extended shifts to make more money.

Many times, a loss of happiness can create some major life tragedies. When a person is no longer happy, hope is one of the first things that floats away. That person has tied everything they are, their whole identity, to a sense of temporary well-being. No foundation is there. Everything just comes crashing down when tragedy strikes. Since society is so crazy about "quick fixes" and momentary solutions, there is no reason why happiness shouldn't be right there leading the way. Society uses happiness as a "feel good" drug and people have pursued it to great lengths and expense. Unfortunately, after many years of pursuing this so called "worldly happiness", what usually ends up happening is that the individual opens their eyes one day and realizes they are still not fulfilled or happy at all.

The money and time wasted are just that, wasted. Chasing after worldly things have proven to be nothing but vanity; they will not make you truly happy. This kind of happiness will never fill that void; only the joy God can give us will. Anything we seek shouldn't be all about us anyway; this includes joy or happiness. That's why scripture says:

"But seek first his kingdom and his righteousness, and all these things will be given to you as well." (Matthew 6:33)

If we go after God and seek everything from Him, He will give us what we need, including joy. Living in joy allows us to honor him, that's why it's so important to let Him give that to you. You will never find it on your own. I can tell you that I am seeking Him every day so I can receive what I can only get from Him.

Even as I write on this topic, I recognize that I still don't have the full joy in which God wants me to have. I have to ask God every day, multiple times to instill in me a "joyful heart". I believe having joy in my heart is one of the greatest catapults towards intentionally doing more for God's kingdom. His joy is what we need!

MY PRAYER: Dear God, I pray that this book in which You have

given me to write will bless those who read it. I know God that I am not able to write about joy from a full experience of it, but I do know that I am a more joyful man today than I was in my past. Back then I was living in hurt, anger, and misery. I was just a mean man. I gave to others what I had. I know that there are other men who will read this and they need to know that You, God, can give them a life filled with joy; Your joy! From reading Your Word, I've learned that there is nothing wrong with being joyful as a man. It doesn't take away any of our masculinity. To the contrary Lord, I believe it makes us more of a man. I pray right now that You can open the eyes of men all around the world so that they can see and understand how being joyful honors You. Thank You, Lord, for what You have done in us so far. I pray that every man who reads this chapter will supernaturally receive this awesome gift from You.

In Jesus' name, AMEN!

CHAPTER 11
KNOCK

"Ask and it will be given to you; seek and you will find; knock and the door will be opened to you. For everyone who asks receives; the one who seeks finds; and to the one who knocks, the door will be opened."

(Matthew 7:7, 8)

Does this passage look familiar? If so, it's because it's the same scripture used in the very first chapter where we discussed "ask". Now we take a look at "knock". I was going to open this chapter up with a "knock, knock" joke, but I figured that would be....a bit, you know – *lame*. LOL!

So, why the word knock? I don't really know at this moment. I was trying to come up with a different word for the letter "k", but as I mentioned before, I have to let God guide me. I must write what He impresses upon me, so there you go. As I was sitting down in a relaxed state of mind, meditating, I sought God for guidance and asked Him what I needed to write about. Out of the blue, something was brought to my remembrance about the word knock that raised my eyebrows.

As a young boy I recall my step-mom introducing us to the Jehovah Witness religion. This was actually my very first knowledge about God. Without going into too many specifics, I simply wanted to share with you one specific that took place every Saturday morning. I think you probably know what it is? Yes, that's right. I got the *opportunity* to *knock* on doors, not just one or two doors, but multiple. This kind of knocking isn't necessarily what we will discuss in this chapter, but I bring it up only because I understand what it takes to keep knocking until the knock is answered.

Some Saturday mornings I went door to door with my mother for a couple of hours and our knocks went unanswered. I knew someone was there, but they just wouldn't answer. As an 11 or 12-year-old, I couldn't understand why people didn't want to hear about God. I was knocking to connect with someone and a majority of the time it was to no avail.

Do any of you feel that way at the moment? Have you ever kept knocking on the door and maybe God doesn't seem to want to answer. It can be very frustrating, I know. When it comes to knocking on heaven's door, I learned something very important the hard way: once you have knocked on His door, you have to be patient. God will open it for you if it is His will, secondly when it's the right time.

What tends to happen a lot of the time is this: we knock, we knock again, and we knock a few more times and the door still doesn't open. What do you do then? Do you knock some more or do you wait it out? Maybe both. But I believe that answer depends on what you think God is impressing upon you. It could also depend on what your accountability partner is telling you about the matter (that's if you have even brought the matter to someone you've been accountable to).

If you have brought the matter before others and they are praying on the matter with you, then maybe God has used someone to speak to you on His behalf. Sometimes it can be very clear that the door will stay closed and never open. One of the worst mistakes we can make is forcing any door open.

I remember some time ago back in Germany, like in 1986, I literally forced a door open and it cost me dearly. I was living with a woman at the time and we fought all the time. On this particular day we were at it again. She had her cousin there at the apartment and she called her brother for him to come and get them. I was so angry that I just left and walked to the bus stop. After a few minutes I saw her brother driving to our apartment so I walked back. Once I got there the door was locked. I knocked and no one answered. I then proceeded to loudly pound on the door, but all that did was draw the attention of the landlord who was downstairs in her office.

I continued to pound on the door, but they wouldn't open it. The three of them pushed against the door from the inside as if they knew I would be able to push the door open. I was so angry. I looked at the owner who was standing on the stairs and I told her that I would pay for any damages, and with one huge heave I pushed open this huge, oak door, deadbolt and all, tearing out all three sets of hinges, as well and toppling it on the three individuals trying to hold it closed. The owner stood there in complete disbelief. The brother left promptly, and all I could do was pick the heavy door back up and try and set it back in place. Needless to say, not only did I have to pay for the damages, but we were also evicted. A little extreme, I know, but I hope you get the point I am trying to make.

You see, it doesn't matter how strong you may be, or how determined, or how smart you think you are; forcing a door open always has consequences. Like I mentioned in the example I just shared, my consequence was being evicted and having to pay a hefty price for the damage done to the door and doorframe.

Because of your determination to force a door open, what have you paid the price for? I believe one of the reasons we do this is because we let our pride get in the way of reason. God is saying "Wait," but your flesh screams, "I want this!", "I need this!", or "I can do this!"

Instead of fasting and praying in the midst of having to wait, you seek to please and gratify the flesh. Why? Is it because it's a good deal? Or because you need to act now before it gets taken away? Or maybe it just makes sense to do it? However you convince yourself to justify your thoughts instead of waiting on Him to open the door, you'll soon realize that it wasn't the right thing to do.

There have been times when it made sense for me to knock and open the door, so I figured, let me go for it. I found out shortly afterwards that I had made a huge mistake not waiting for God to open it for me; or at least letting Him guide me to the correct door. Sometimes I have been pretty far in until I realized that it was the wrong door that I had knocked on. Then another set of confusion sets in. I asked myself back then, "How could the door be opened if it wasn't the right door to begin with?"

Remember we still have an enemy trying to prevent us from doing anythIng that God has intended for us, so that's another crucial reason why we must make sure our opportunities are from God. I believe if we take our own thoughts, solutions, and reasoning out of the equation, it becomes easier to hear from God when He is trying to show us the right door to knock on. Let me remind you of a very important scripture to help us with this.

"For my thoughts are not your thoughts, neither are your ways my ways," declares the Lord. "As the heavens are higher than the earth, so are my ways higher than your ways and my thoughts than your thoughts." (Isaiah 55:8, 9)

At the beginning of this chapter, I mentioned my door-to-door experiences as a Jehovah's Witness. There is more to that experience. How about the experience of having literal doors slammed in my face?!

Uh, it can happen to you too if it hasn't already.

Sometimes if you open a door by force God can slam it shut right in your face. Has this happened to you? You're going along just living life when you think everything is good, believing that it was definitely God who opened this door for you when all of a sudden, slam! You're stunned and even maybe somewhat confused. You're like, "What the heck just happened? I must have done something wrong and this is my punishment."

The only thing you did wrong was not wait on God to open the right door for you. This has definitely happened to me on more than one occasion. God loves you and I so much that He wants the best for us. So when He does slam the door closed before we get in too deep, be thankful. The reason why I say this is because sometimes the door can no longer be closed because you are in too deep. God used all kinds of signs to show you that you've gone through the wrong door, but since it "all made sense" and "looked good" you didn't see or hear any of the warning signs. You know what I'm talking about. Us guys know this all too well. Because God is God and we are not, He has a solution for that too. It's found here in Romans 8:28.

"And we know that in all things God works for the good of those who love him, who have been called according to his purpose."

It says, "In all things God works for the good of those who love Him." This means even when we mess up and knock on the wrong doors, or date the wrong women, or accept the wrong positions, He still works it all out. Have you experienced this first hand? I know I have, otherwise I surely would not be writing this chapter right now.

I have gone knocking on too many wrong doors, opening several with my own strength. I have learned throughout the years that doors open so much easier when you have keys; keys to unlock the doors that only God can give us. These are very special keys. Have you watched the movie, *The Matrix Reloaded*? Well, at the infancy stage of my Christianity, I did. Anyway, do you remember the Key Maker? Neo has to find the Key Maker to access a multidimensional door to the Architect, who is also credited as the initial source of the Matrix. Neo needs one specific key to get into that one specific door. Think about it, if we have the key, then why do we need to knock?

The key is what God gives to us when we stand before the door and knock. I believe if you are in His will and you are knocking at the right door, then He will hand you the specific key to enter and walk through. How many keys do you have on your key ring? Are there some that you have no idea what they go to? To help you, let me suggest that you remove all the keys that have no place and keep only the keys that you believe in your heart that God wants you to use.

In the context of knocking, this is a persistent prayer for the advancement of God's purpose and plan in all areas of your life. Answer this question:

Do you believe in the goodness of God to the point where you will persist in asking Him?

MY PRAYER:

Heavenly Father, I pray right now in the name of Jesus, that men everywhere would know and understand that we need only knock and the promise is that You will give to us what we need. Knocking on your door Lord is not about receiving what we want but receiving what You know we need. We don't ever have to worry about knocking and you asking, "who is there"? You already know even before we come and knock. The promise is in Your word. You say, Lord "...and to the one who knocks, the door will be opened". You are a good God and want only what's best for each and every one of us. I pray Lord, that we men would come boldly and knock with purpose so that the door will be opened and we can then walk through the door of opportunity that is meant for us. I pray that we would not give up so easily if the door doesn't open right away. We have to learn to keep knocking until we get to the right door that is meant for each of us. Thank you for patience, perseverance, obedience, and all of the topics in this book that can help us get to where you are trying to take us! Thank you so much Lord!

In Jesus' name, AMEN!

CHAPTER 12

LOVE L

"Love is patient, love is kind. It does not envy, it does not boast, it is not proud. It does not dishonor others, it is not self-seeking, it is not easily angered, it keeps no record of wrongs. Love does not delight in evil but rejoices with the truth. It always protects, always trusts, always hopes, and always perseveres. Love never fails. But where there are prophecies, they will cease; where there are tongues, they will be stilled; where there is knowledge, it will pass away."

(1 Corinthians 13:4-8)

Ok, before I go any further, I have to confess something to you guys. I have been trying to figure out how to avoid writing this chapter; actually, to be specific, this topic. I know there are other words that begin with the letter "L" that I could write about, right? As I mentioned previously, this book has to be and is going to be completely led by what God impresses upon me to write. Every time I feel the desire to change a topic, I am quickly reminded of who is in charge here. It's not me, but Him. All right, I said it. Let's keep it moving along.

Here I am, one of the last people on earth that should be writing on the topic of love. No, I'm serious. But here I am writing on something that I probably still don't completely have a grasp of. Really, do any of us? It wasn't until God came into my life that I began to understand anything about love. Oh sure, I've heard the word ever since I can remember. I have used it myself quite often, but I never really knew what love was until I met God. While meeting God, I learned what love was and still is through the heart of a woman who would later become my wife, Carrie. God used her to show me love, help me to receive love, and learn to give love as well.

When I met Carrie, I had absolutely no idea that God would show me these things. Before I get into that story, let's discuss a few other things first. How about this: Where are you with understanding love? What do you understand it to be? I know that men struggle with this more than women do because of how society has put a spin on love and masculinity. However, another issue when it comes to men and love is the fact that a lot of us were never shown love, or how to give love, or in many situations how to even receive love. Are any of you saying amen to that?

I surely am!

When you read my testimony at the end of this book you will see specifically how I grew up. This is not to point fingers and put blame on our parents about what they did or didn't do. No. I believe the fact of the matter today is that our parents probably did the best they could with what they were given. Either way, a person can only do or give what they have or are able to give.

I forgave my parents a long time ago as part of my own healing process. If you haven't forgiven your parents as of now, I strongly suggest that you do before going any further. If it wasn't your parents who hurt you, then forgive whoever it was. You are going to need to forgive them for your own healing. Although I forgave my parents, we still don't have a healthy relationship. I've tried and tried, but I believe their own issues and guilt keeps them from receiving my forgiveness. Like I said though, forgiving them was for my healing, not theirs.

By God's grace, I was even able to tell them from my heart that I love them, even if they didn't receive it. Looking back, I was able to do so because I could see how my parents tried to show me love, although it was the only way they knew how. I never got the hugs and kisses growing up, but that's only part of it. That aspect of love is more so showing affection, which is more about the expression of care. What I

have learned about love is that love is more of an action than a feeling. Love is more about what you do, rather than what you get. The type of

love that society teaches us is more about "feel good" stuff. If something feels right or feels good, then you are experiencing love. When the "feel good" has worn off, then it's bye, bye baby. This kind of love I know all too well. Love in its purest form has nothing to do with "feelings," it has everything to do with "doing". Look at the opening scripture again:

"Love is patient, love is kind. It does not envy, it does not boast, it is not proud. It does not dishonor others, it is not self-seeking, it is not easily angered, it keeps no record of wrongs. Love does not delight in evil but rejoices with the truth. It always protects, always trusts, always hopes, and always perseveres. Love never fails. But where there are prophecies, they will cease; where there are tongues, they will be stilled; where there is knowledge, it will pass away"
(1 Corinthians 13:4-8).

Do you get it? Read it again. Read it aloud. Are you getting it? Naw, you don't get it yet. Let me finish the story I started earlier about Carrie. The reason I want to share this with you is because from the beginning I knew nothing about love. But when God brought Carrie my way, He began to show me everything; everything being things that He had promised me years before.

So, Carrie hired me in 2002 as the hotel property security. I had originally turned this position down because I was a bouncer in Latin clubs and living pretty well by doing so. At this time my marriage of 12 years was falling apart and I had been living multiple lives. I had several affairs with many women and men. My sex life was way out of control and my wife had no clue. It wasn't until I got arrested one night and left my cell phone on the table due to an argument. My wife at the time found out about one of the women I was seeing and after I was bonded out of jail, I got kicked out of the apartment. I had no choice but to take the job that was offered to me a couple of weeks prior.

As you have already figured out, although I used the word often, love was nowhere in my world. It wouldn't be until I met this woman named Carrie that I begin to learn and understand what love is. As I mentioned earlier, God was about to use this woman to show me true love; of course I had no clue of it. I was living on the hotel property with a woman I had gotten pregnant during one of my affairs. I had two sons already with my wife and another one with my mistress. I did some very crazy things for this woman. Not only did I supposedly "love" her, but I was "in love" with her as well.

Stefen was born in March of 2002 and we moved onto the property a few months later in July. I would say from summer of 2002 to sometime in 2004, I lived a very confused and sex filled life. I was trying to fill this "love" void, or rather the lack of. I was living alone now and I had begun sleeping with Carrie as well as my son's mother and even my wife who I was still separated from. I also continued a pursuit of sexual relations with men as well. I was completely out of control. I had a few fetishes that I acted out on also. For some time, I went through a "big woman" phase and this is where Carrie fit in. Carrie, at the time was a fairly large woman, what they call a BBW, or Big Beautiful Woman, and she had four kids! Carrie and I not only had sex but we talked a lot. I mean a whole lot. She would share Bible verses with me and talk a lot about God. She was the one who taught me the most about God. I thought I was just going to fulfill a fetish and move on to the next; but God had other plans. Carrie and I started living together in 2004 and we have been together ever since. Being with Carrie was different than being with anyone else I had ever been with, including my ex-wife. I had no clue what it was. I can tell you this: even though I fought our relationship all the way for many years, we somehow stayed together.

I have told myself so often that I did not want to be with Carrie and her four kids. But it was like I had no control over the situation or my decisions. It was kind of weird actually. Although I was still married to my then wife, yet living in sin with Carrie, God somehow was still orchestrating my future. It was as if a different aspect of our relationship fell into place at a time. It surely didn't seem that way back then though. But with hindsight, we see how God put everything together. My wife at the time had filed for divorce and it was finalized in August 2006. Carrie, the kids and I had been attending church already for a year by the time my divorce was complete and I had already surrendered my life over to God.

During the time of me being born again, I remember God impressing upon me to stay with Carrie and the kids. If I did so He would show me "marvelous things". I never really understood what that meant, but there we were in 2006 and I was still fighting the fact that I "had" to be with Carrie and her four kids. I remember back in 2004 I tried to be with another woman whom I had worked with at another hotel, and I would make up lies so that I could be with her just because I didn't want to be with Carrie. But once again, God stepped in. I mean it could have only been Him. I tried having sex with this woman and "it" didn't want to work! What! I have never had that problem. We tried it a few times and the best I ever got was a half erection. I mean I couldn't believe it. Then Carrie figured out what was going on and confronted me. That would be the first and last time I would ever try and cheat on Carrie.

I sat around trying to figure out why "it" didn't work because "it" worked fine with Carrie. What I came up with was that Carrie was God's special woman. I called her God's angel and God was making sure that nothing or no one separated what He was putting together. Carrie and I would become a very special couple. Even to this day, I believe that Carrie is God's special angel and that I am not allowed to do her any harm or I'll have to deal with God. What God wanted to do was show me "love" from a woman, not "sex-love". You know where you confuse the good feelings of sex with "love". That's one of men's biggest issues.

Up until August 2006 I often wondered why I was still with Carrie and why she was still with me. Carrie had her own voices to deal with; voices telling her to get out while she could. I was very abusive to her; more verbal than physical. I was abusive to her children. Why would she stay with me? I wouldn't stay with me. I was a very mean and angry man. Why would God allow this relationship to go on? I thought it was only going to lead to something very bad. If I truly believed that, then what happened next should have sealed the "failure" deal.

In the midst of all this mess and chaos God did the most presumable thing ever. I was walking from the living room toward the front door when I believe the Holy Spirit tells me, "Now is the time." No kidding. I remember it like it was yesterday. He then said it again, "Now is the time."

I was like, "Time for what?" Then it hit me. I became nauseous and a little lightheaded. It didn't make any sense to me. It hasn't even been a week since my divorce was made final and now I'm supposed to jump right back into it again? "But Lord, I don't love Carrie." I told Him. "Aren't two people supposed to get married because they love each other?" Then He reminded me of the promise He made to me a few years earlier. He told me that He would show me "marvelous things".

So as a disclaimer guys, don't let your wives read this next section, because they might just take this book away from you. You'll see why in a second. You see, I didn't propose, I had no ring; both Carrie and I had recently lost our jobs and on top of that we had no car! I hadn't even taken Carrie out on a first date! I am so serious. I definitely wouldn't say that we were in the best shape to be getting married.

So yes, there it is. God impressed upon me to get married to Carrie that day, that time, no waiting allowed! On August 8, 2006 at around 2:00 pm I went upstairs and simply told Carrie that it was time. Of course, she looked at me funny and wanted to know time for what? All I could tell her was, you know, we have to do that "thing". She stood there for a minute and it hit her. "Oh, now?" She asked.

What a way to lift a girl off her feet, huh? You see why I don't want your wives reading this part? They probably would be furious. I can tell you that if I could do it all over again, I would do everything the exactly the same way! Yes, I would. Why? Even in the midst of my bad attitude, God showed up in a huge way. He completely took over and made something awesome happen!

By August 24, 2006 Carrie and I were married at the courthouse. Now without my knowledge, Carrie had always wanted one special thing to happen at her wedding. She didn't get it at her first wedding, but God hadn't forgotten about her. He was about to show up yet again! When the judge went to sit down he looked up at us and said, "I am not technically supposed to do what I am about to do, however I feel a strong prompting to do so." He then proceeded to pick up the Bible and turn to Matthew 19:4-6 which he read aloud over us. Carrie burst into tears, she was floored that this happened without any interference from either of us. Here's what that verse says:

"Haven't you read," he replied, "that at the beginning the Creator 'made them male and female,' and said, 'For this reason a man will leave his father and mother and be united to his wife, and the two will become one flesh'? So they are no longer two, but one flesh. Therefore what God has joined together, let no one separate." (Matthew 19:4-6)

Although we didn't have a fancy wedding with guests and all, what we did have was so powerful. I mean God was right there in our midst showing us the beginning of "marvelous things". I knew from that day, without a shadow of a doubt, that He had orchestrated the whole thing;

all the way back to when Carrie hired me at White Columns Inn in July of 2002. I knew from that moment standing before the judge, I was going to have to step it up and learn how to love this woman that God had given me. I had to start receiving her love first and foremost and at the same time, love her as Christ loves the Church. Of course, back then I really didn't understand what that even looked like, but at least I saw and felt some major changes happening within me and around me.

Throughout the years I could see more of those "marvelous things" happening in our lives. I knew that God loved me. I knew that Carrie and the kids loved me, and honestly I was getting much better at loving them as well. I also believe that God made it to where the very first serving ministry I would be involved with would be serving the homeless. There's nothing like learning to love on the last, the least, and the lost in the streets. There are so many stories that I could share with you on how God has worked in my life; showing me what love is. It really began when He used this amazing woman; Carrie and her four kids going through a very difficult time to just love *me*.

In return, I can only love others and give the love that I have been shown. I can say this because now I know that God is the source of love. I share this particular love story with you because it had such a profound impact on my life. This was the beginning of learning about God and His amazing love.

What I have learned throughout life is that you have to be willing to receive love from Him, your wife, and even those around you. You can't go through life "love-less" like I did for so many wandering years. If you think you can't give or receive love, it's a lie. Yes, that is true! It's a lie and here's why:

"So God created mankind in his own image, in the image of God he created them; male and female he created them." (Genesis 1:27)

God created mankind in His own image. Think about that. The only way you cannot love is because you *don't* know Him. But if you *do* know Him, saying that you are not capable of giving or receiving love is a lie because God is love.

"Whoever does not love does not know God, because God is love."
(1 John 4:8)

I believe then, the closer I am to God and the stronger relationship I have with Him, the more I am capable of receiving love from Him; which in turn, I am able to pass on to others. In my story, I couldn't love because I didn't have a relationship with God. It was honestly the toughest thing in the world. It wasn't until I received Him as my Lord and Savior and surrendered to Him that my life was able to show signs of love. Although I can say that I didn't stay with Carrie out of love for her, there must've been something buried deep inside of me that made me stay.

You see, from the beginning of creation, God doesn't force us to make decisions, we have free will. Was there love in my spirit that kept Carrie and I together, or was Carrie's love for me enough to keep us together? I doubt it. There is never enough love inside of any human being for that to happen. I had to step up and receive what I needed from God which was His love. All I know is this: at first I didn't love at all, and then I did love. Now I can admit to complete strangers that my love has grown stronger over the years and it is because of Christ. As my relationship with God gets stronger, so does my love for my wife and others.

When it comes to the topic of love, you have got to stop letting people make excuses for you in this matter. You know, when your wife or maybe your kids say things like, "He loves us in his own way," or "He shows love differently than others". No, no, no. This can't keep going on. If you are really truthful about the matter, let me ask you this question; is "your way" of showing love working? I bet not! It can't. You know why? Because it's simply not possible. Anything we try to do in our own ability never works out long-term and loving people without God's input definitely doesn't either.

You might be thinking, *well, my way has worked for me*. Good for you! Guess what though, it's not about you. You can't keep going on in life creating your own definitions of something because it makes you feel safe. Everything that we try and create or reinvent ourselves never works! It doesn't fill the voids that are there within us; it doesn't. Look around, and tell me what do you see? Everybody is chasing after the same thing, but everyone is trying to do it with their own recipes, but don't you see it doesn't work that way?

To love, we must learn from the example that has been set before us by the One who created love. We must learn from the One who is love. Every manufacturer of something has instruction manuals on how to use their products. Why wouldn't the creator of humanity have the same, especially since He created the world in which we were placed? He is the author and creator of life. He is the only way to doing things the right way. Forget trying to love someone your way. Something so delicate, something so important deserves the respect of learning to do it the right way. Love is about others. To give is to receive.

I wrote earlier in this chapter that I had to learn to receive love first. In order to know love, to know what it looks like, to know what it tastes like and feels like, I had to see it in action first. I didn't know what love really was, remember? Once I was able to identify with it, I could then give it and receive it in its fullness. Am I making sense? You can't give something away to someone that you yourself don't yet have. That is why it is so very important to learn love from God and not what society says it is.

Check out the differences in the two meanings. The first is what the dictionary defines love to be:

- a feeling of strong or constant affection for a person
- attraction that includes sexual desire
- the strong affection felt by people who have a romantic relationship
- a person you love in a romantic way

Here's what I found the biblical definition of love to be:

Purposeful commitment to sacrificial action for another.

bible-truth.org, "The Biblical Meaning of Love" by Cooper Abrams

It goes on to say this: Powerful emotions may accompany love, but it is the commitment of the will that holds true biblical love steadfast and unchanging.

Is this dictionary definition wrong?

No, not necessarily. In order for love to be complete, you need the biblical definition more so than the dictionary version. The dictionary version is just incomplete. Feelings, whether strong or just mild, come and go. Today I love you, tomorrow I won't. That's just not love. I could go on and on writing about love, but this book wasn't supposed to be about love only. There are so many books on love that if you would just take some time to research, you could see some things that just might help as well. What I hope that you receive from this chapter is pretty simple. Open yourself up to the possibility that you can receive love and you can give love the way God intended for you to. All you have to do is be committed to fully surrendering your life to Him so that He can show you.

MY PRAYER:

Heavenly Father, I thank You for this chapter on love. I pray that I have put down what You wanted me to and that those who read it are blessed. May they be blessed as much, if not more, than I have been in writing these words. I pray Lord that men can learn to humble themselves so they can receive this glorious gift of love. I thank You for everyday that You continue to show men and teach men about love. My prayer is that we may be able to love our wife as Christ loves the Church, and that I can love my neighbor as myself. But first teach us how to love our self. Father, take away the things that have caused men's hearts to harden; the pain and suffering from the past. I pray they would fully understand and grasp how much You love them so they may in return go and love the way Your Word says, not the way the world says. May Your will be done.

In Jesus' name, AMEN!

CHAPTER (13)

MATURE (M)

"Let perseverance finish its work so that you may be mature and complete, not lacking anything." (James 1:4)

This chapter is going to be fun, or maybe not so much. I mean since there are so many grown and mature men out there, right? I guess by the time we get to the end of this chapter we will see if any of this applies to you. Don't get upset or start pouting on me if it does. Ha. Just kidding! No, really I'm serious. If it does apply to you, just be open to the idea that you might have some maturity issues. I know I do.

What does it mean to be mature? It might be different for each of you.

Let's take a look though and see what we come up with.
A few definitions of the word *mature* are as follows:

- to become fully developed in the body and mind.

- to continue developing to a desired level.

- to bring to maturity or completion.

- having or showing the mental and emotional qualities of an adult.

- having reached a final or desired state.

Here is something else I found:

It seems that we as a society have forgotten some important values, and are generally becoming more immature as a result. There doesn't seem to be a differentiation between manliness and egocentric chauvinist behavior in a lot of people's minds, which is truly sad. You have people saying things like 30 is the new 20, and grown men acting like entitled spoiled children. The truth is that once you've stepped into your mid-20s you should have gained enough life experience to be able to behave like a mature adult. – lifehack.org.

So, what do you think about this statement? Do you agree or disagree? I believe it to be pretty accurate. What I really want to focus on here is more about the maturity to step up and do what I consider "the hard things". This is where your maturity shows itself. Are you capable of doing things because it's the right thing to do regardless of your feelings? Have you ever said underneath your breath while folding your arms and whining, "I don't want to"? Well that is a sign of immaturity.

I'm sure you probably have your own understanding of what mature means, so I'll just share with you some of my personal experiences on this topic. I believe one of the takeaways from this chapter is going to be on the fact that being mature is more about choices. A mature man "does" because it's the "right" thing to do. No gray area there. Therefore our decisions as men, and as leaders, are based on foundational values, and we stick to those no matter if the tough gets going, or if it's too hot in the kitchen, or if you just don't feel like it. You "do" and "are" because it's the right thing.

I remember one particular time during my relationship with Carrie, before we were married, I had to mature big time with one major situation. It was a very bad and scary situation for us. This was such a huge test for me during my early days as a Christian. Back in March of 2005, Carrie and I took a job together at this hotel chain in a city called Forest Park, which is in Georgia. Carrie was the general manager and she hired me as the chief engineer. We should've known that something was up, but we didn't pay too much attention at first. Without going into too many details about it; most of the staff was stealing money. I mean from Carrie's boss to the front desk clerks. They had a scheme going on where they were all pocketing money from the company. Carrie would catch this and she would start letting people go. I guess the second in charge was the assistant manager who Carrie tried to fire but she couldn't. This was a big problem. Carrie and I talked about what we should do and who we could talk to about it, but we couldn't trust anyone because we didn't know how far up the chain this stealing scheme went.

Honestly, we both should've just left, but we were living way above our means at this point and we couldn't find a job quick enough if we wanted to. It would not have mattered anyway because on one particular Monday morning Carrie took a deposit to the bank, like she always did every morning, and I actually rode with her. Later that day Carrie's boss called her into the office and asked about the deposit. They actually tried to say she never made a deposit and that she stole $14,000! I was so angry; I wanted to put a hurting on that guy! They actually set her up! Of course, Carrie was fired, and so was I. Because of my security background I uncovered some legal stuff going on as well, so they had to get rid of me too.

So, let me skip ahead. There we were, both of us out of work again. Our whole crew pulled together and started cutting grass and doing landscape work in our neighborhood to try and pay our bills. It was a very tough time, but we stuck together as a family and to this day, I continue to do whatever I need to do in order to make ends meet. Finally, in August 2005 Carrie got a job with a magazine company and I was building out basements and things were starting to pick up a little. We kept our faith in God and he was really showing himself in a big way.

A few months later in November I got the phone call. I'm covered in drywall dust and on the other line there was this detective. The detective on the case told me that Carrie had been arrested at her office and that she was being processed in Clayton County for felony theft. It felt like all of my blood had just drained out of my body. I have never felt that way in my life! I literally fell to my knees and cried like I have never cried before. I am actually choking up right now as I'm writing this. This was the day of devastation. We had no money to post bond, we had nothing of value to sell to get the money to post bond. I didn't have any family that would help and Carrie's family couldn't do anything either. We were definitely at a dead-end.

At this point, Carrie's kids stepped up and became front and center. There were three boys and one girl between ages of 11 and 16. The daughter was the oldest of the four. I can tell you that I did not want any part of this! I was just about as done as one could be. I began trying to figure out my exit strategy. I called Carrie's dad and he said that he wouldn't take the kids. I called our church and one of the leaders on staff recommended I let DFACS pick them up. I mean, I had no legal guardianship over these kids. I had no clue what to do if something happened to one of them. There were so many school issues and papers to sign. I was worried about being alone with the teenage girl and what I could get accused of.

All these crazy thoughts were going through my head and I didn't know what to do. Although I didn't have a very good relationship with my parents, I figured I could put up with them before having to go through

this crap. So, I called my dad and told him what had happened. To my surprise he suggested that I come to Virginia with them until I can figure it all out. Yes! I had a way out of this mess!

Did I mention earlier in this book that God's ways are not my ways and His thoughts not my thoughts? Yeah, I'm pretty sure I did. Since we are discussing the topic of maturity, do you think my actions have been mature so far? Hey, I mean, I wasn't married to Carrie, and there was no kind of agreement or commitment, right? On top of all that we were being evicted, so why not just quietly leave all that behind me and get going to Virginia? So as the story is told, I packed my bags. My church's small-group night was coming up, so I decided to go ahead and go. I needed to let my circle of church family know what happened to Carrie and what I was planning to do.

The group leaders, Dale and Yemi asked me to pray and really think it over and they wanted to come by the house the next evening to see if anything had changed. I agreed to do so. After small group I went back home and tried to figure this thing out. I was angry with Carrie's dad. I was angry at the church for just telling me to call DFACS so they could just take the kids. I was battling back-and-forth about all these feelings and also about having to choose what was right. I was angry at others for not doing what was right, but yet I couldn't do what was right. This was the moment when "maturity" was staring me down and I wanted no part of it.

At that time I can promise you one thing, making a mature decision was certainly not on my mind. I just wanted out. I remember that night crying over the kitchen sink and Morgan, the oldest, put her hand on my back and comforted me by saying in her sweet voice, "Everything will be just fine." A 16-year-old girl told me that everything was going to be just fine. She had no idea what was going to happen to her brothers, to her, or even her mother, but everything was going to be just fine, huh?

The next evening Dale, the leader from my small group, and Yemi showed up and we discussed options. They told me that whatever I decided to do that they would help wherever he could. They never really told me what I should or shouldn't do. As we talked, the answer on what to do seemed to be getting clearer. I kept defending the kids. I kept telling them that it was wrong to give them over to DFACS, and on top of that when their mother did get out, she would have a heck of a time getting them back. All I saw was more heartache for Carrie if I did the wrong thing. I kept asking what God wanted me to do, but He never really said anything. I felt moved by what he told me. Dale said this, "Richard, if you decide to take on this challenge of keeping the kids, myself and the rest of the group will help you. You can depend on us to help you."

"I don't know," I shared, "I don't think I can do this."

I could either mature quickly or tuck my tail between my legs and run. Isn't that what happens to us most of the time? You are faced with a huge situation and you just sweep it under the rug because you don't "feel" like dealing with it or maybe you just hand it off to someone else, or worse case, you actually run away from it? I think I know why you respond that way. Could it be you don't even know how to handle the situation? Perhaps you completely don't know what to do so you get scared and become fearful? That's how teenagers, young adults, and unfortunately even adults that have not yet matured respond to situations. Did you catch that? The reason why you respond the way you do to situations is because you have not yet fully matured.

Obstacles and challenges in life are all about teaching us

to mature. We really can't teach someone to mature, but we can show them their choices on how to handle situations that arise. Maturity has absolutely nothing to do with your age. Look around; you have 40-year-old men that *should* be very mature, still making immature decisions and it is costing them every day. Going after the "fountain of youth", and reverting back to how they were in their youth. Acting like a 20-year-old at 40 is not very cool at all. That doesn't keep you young, by the way. Look, I'm not talking about how one dresses or what they decide to drive around in. I'm talking about the maturity level that tells you what is appropriate at your age and what is not. This is the same maturity that tells you which decisions should be made according to what is right.

Since I just brought up decisions, you're probably wondering what decision I made with Carrie and her kids. After Dale and Yemi prayed with me, I felt an ease come over me. I felt that God was present at that moment and that He wanted me to stay. It was like He was telling me the same thing Morgan told me in the kitchen a few days prior, that everything will be fine. I just needed to hand it over to Him and He would see us through this mess. So that's what I did. I finally chose to become a mature man. I won't go into what all happened after I made the decision to stay, but I will tell you the temperature in the kitchen increased tremendously. That however, will have to wait for another time. The point I was trying to make with this story or testimony is there comes a time when "play time" comes to an end and we have to step up and become mature men. There comes a time when we need to make mature and wise decisions for the benefit of our families. God can't use men that still have recess on their minds. We can't keep running away from maturing. More and more situations will arise to test us and to grow us. Take a look at these verses:

"Consider it pure joy, my brothers and sisters, whenever you face trials of many kinds, because you know that the testing of your faith produces perseverance. Let perseverance finish its work so that you may be mature and complete, not lacking anything." (James 1: 2-4)

Verse 4 was the chapter verse because it tells us that when we persevere through our situations, trials, and obstacles we become mature. So instead of running away or handing them off to someone else, seek God for the answers on what to do. He will help you in the way He sees necessary. God never said that we had to have all the answers. One thing I've learned however is where to get the answers and that's what I want to pass on to you. God can tell you directly or He can use others like He used Dale, Yemi and Morgan in my decision of maturity. All you have to do when you can't do anymore, or you don't even know what to do, is stand. Just stand still and ask the One who can do it all!

MY PRAYER:
Heavenly Father,

What an amazing topic You had me write on. Thank You, for my testimony that You allowed me to share with all who read this. Lord, my prayer is simple. I pray for men to just stand; stand still and let You work it all out on their behalf. God, You are so great that even when we try and make a mature decision, but end up making the wrong one, You still work it all out for the good of those who love you! So, Lord I want the men to know this, no worries! Encourage them not to be afraid to mature. May we let You, the Author and Creator, show us how to mature Your way, not the world's way. Lord, I know that You are still working in us to become more mature every day, but as long as we stay close to You, we will mature into the men that You intend for us to be, and so will all the other teenagers and young men who are lacking maturity. God, I speak a spirit of maturity over each and every man that reads this prayer. I pray that You will show men the areas that still requires more maturing so that they can be better husbands to their wives, better fathers to their children, better leaders at work, in the church or wherever you place them. I pray for the hearts of the men worldwide to be open and receive whatever it is You want them receive in this book and with this particular chapter. Thank You!

In Jesus' name, AMEN!

CHAPTER 14
NEW

"Therefore, if anyone is in Christ, *the new creation has come*: The old has gone, the new is here." (2 Corinthians 5:17)

In July 2014 Carrie and I went to the dealership to see about possibly trading in our 2010 Dodge Journey or possibly refinancing it to a lower payment. We quickly found out that there wasn't going to be any refinancing, even though the sales manager told us to come back in a year when we first bought it. Hmmh, car salesman! What they did tell us was that we could go ahead and get a new car, but we would have to keep the Journey or......you know, hint, hint. They didn't say it outright but he was insinuating we could let the Journey go back. Basically default on the loan. The good thing was Trey, Carrie's oldest son needed a car and he was working so maybe he would take over payments. The car they wanted us to buy was this black on black 2014 Dodge Avenger. It sure looked pretty cool, shiny black paint with black rims! That would make for a great Man On Purpose vehicle if you ask me.

After a few hours, we drove out of there with a brand new car that had only 8 miles on the odometer! It had that "new" car smell and everything. Of course it did, it was brand new! No shoes, no eating, no dogs, no anything inside of this "new" car of ours. We had to do things different now with this car because it was "new". Do you get where I am going with this? Did you read the chapter scripture verse? This is a topic that a lot of people seem to think is open for debate. What does it mean to be NEW in Christ? That's exactly what we are going to explore in this chapter. I am just as curious as you are to see where the Lord leads me with this one.

"Do not lie to each other, since you have taken off your old self with its practices, and have *put on the new self*, which is being renewed in knowledge in the image of its Creator." (Colossians 3:9,10)

I remember when I finally gave my life over to Christ, I knew what I was getting myself into. I didn't however know the exact course to follow, but I knew some kind of change would happen. That's why on that Saturday night something inside of me yearned for change and whatever it was knew that God was the way. The next day, off to church we went to find Him. It didn't stop with just going to church though, I am sure you are pretty well aware of that. Maybe some of you are.

I know that some of you reading this might not have received the revelation quite yet that you have to do more than just "show up". In order for the *new you* to spring forth, you have to work on getting rid of the *old you*. You know the selfish, prideful, lustful, greedy you. The you that did whatever he wanted to whenever he wanted to no matter the consequences. That sounds a bit like something we discussed in the previous chapter, just sayin'.

"You were taught, with regard to your former way of life, to *put off your old self*, which is being corrupted by its deceitful desires; to be made new in the attitude of your minds; and to *put on the new self*, created to be like God in true righteousness and holiness."
(Ephesians 4:22-24)

If you notice in all of these verses it tells us "to do" something. Remember we discussed DO in chapter 4, which encompasses every single chapter and topic. None of these will work unless you are actively involved in your change. I don't know about you, but I like new things. It doesn't matter what it is. I like new clothes, or new electronics, new places, or new days. New is just that - new. It's fresh out of the package; no one else has touched it. You are the first! You open a new package of coffee, so full of aroma, isn't that an amazing smell? Well, it is to me. Think about what you like new. How does it make you feel? Don't you want to always take extra good care of that new something? I remember when I got the brand new iPad mini. I put it into a LIFEPROOF case right away so that nothing would happen to it. What about you?

I mentioned a few paragraphs back that I counted the cost when I gave my life over to Jesus. I knew that change was going to happen. What I didn't know was how that change was going to happen. I don't remember, but I'm sure I didn't think I was going to say a prayer and BAM, all would change. I hope none of you think that's how it happens, 'cause if you do, I'm here to tell you that you will be let down. But, I'm sure you already knew that.

I don't know about you, but I am not afraid of new. Some of you might be however. You try and figure out what the new will look like and the more you try and figure it out the more you cling onto the old. The old is familiar. It's amazing how people will hold onto the old even though it's broken or it smells really bad; so bad that washing it twice still won't take the stink out.

Sometimes people think they will lose their identities, kinda like the witness relocation program. You know what, yes it's exactly like that! Having a new identity in Christ is exactly like getting put into the witness relocation program. The biggest difference is that you don't have to change your name or address, or anything. You do however take on a completely different role. You can't go to the same places anymore. You can't hang around the same people anymore. In some cases you can't even dress the same way anymore. You have to change the old you into a completely different new you. It's called "transformation".

You see, God created you with a vision and a plan for your life. He knows everything He wants you to do. If you believe that, then why are you so easily influenced to be someone different? Do you remember when you were a teenager and you struggled with identity issues and tried to fit in? What did most of us do? We played into the crowd, peer pressure and all. Go back and look at old photos of yourself. How many different hairstyles did you have? How many clothing styles did you have? You see, you followed what everyone else was doing. For 99% of us, our style was not our own, it was what everyone else was doing. God's style would have lasted through all those temporary styles.

If you were anything like me, you probably weren't even a Christ follower back in your hay day. I'm only trying to get you to see what God really wanted for you and for me, but we didn't know any better. The thing is this: once you "know" better, you "do" better, right? Isn't that the mature thing to do? Then why are there so many men who refuse to change? I understand struggling with change, but there are some of you who recently decided that what you are doing in life was not good enough. You finally said, "I'm not comfortable with where I'm at in life right now." Fortunately, a bright future can still be attained.

New is good! But is becoming new easy? Nope. I don't recall reading that anywhere in the Bible, especially changing into someone new. Here's what you need to understand. This one simple tidbit is the answer to the question, how? How do we change into something new? First thing we need to realize is that it's not all of our doing. It's a partnership that gets the job done. It's us and God. That's right. It's God that changes us! That's what makes it so sad when men refuse to become new. They stay the way they are for years because they see change as being too hard. They haven't reached the maturity to understand and know that becoming a new creation in Christ is all about letting God do the changing. All we have to do is the seeking, asking, and doing. You don't even have to know specifically what needs to change to become new. God will show you. He has to show us, do you know why? It's because there is so much that needs to change, we wouldn't know where to begin. God knows what He wants you to work on and exactly when. If you have surrendered your life and have a relationship with Him, then you'll know your part to play in this life changing experience.

Have you ever heard a sermon or teaching on a certain subject and it felt like the pastor was speaking directly to you? Like maybe your wife went and had a discussion with him and that's how he knew? Funny! Me too. That's God trying to tell you that it's time to work on whatever the teaching was about. Now then, it's up to you to do something with that. Are you supposed to just go home and not think about the message anymore? No! You are supposed to take action and sign up for that marriage class. You are supposed to take action and break the chains of bondage. Go ahead and walk up to the man behind that Celebrate Recovery kiosk in the lobby.

Do you take moments like these as hints or nudges from God or do you merely shrug them off? I remember one of the very first serving ministries that Carrie and I served in came about in a very similar way. While at Victory World Church, Pastor Dennis was teaching on serving and he brought up some of the areas to serve in. The Mercy Team was one of them. Well, Carrie and I already had a great amount of dealings with the homeless people. Remember when I told you that Carrie hired me in 2002? Well, it was a very rundown, extended stay, crack hotel. These people were considered some of the last, least, and lost in society. There were prostitutes, addicts, dealers, gang bangers, you name it. These people were on the property every day and every night. My job was to rid the property of the so-called infestation. It took a couple of years, but eventually we would have a pretty clean and decent living environment.

Now, I'll be honest, how that came about was of course a lot of violence. Then as God would have it, a shift began to happen. I found myself sitting down with these people and we would share life stories. We literally shared our struggles together. I didn't even realize this until Carrie and I talked about it much later. Then this opportunity came about to become part of the Mercy Team and serve with the 7 Bridges to Recovery ministry. This was the best ministry we could've been a part of to go and love on the homeless in downtown Atlanta, particularly under the bridges where a lot of these people lived! I know I already discussed my issues about learning to love etc., but I believe God was setting this opportunity up for us to both get involved in this, or not.

I say or not, because it was still my choice whether I wanted to get involved in something that could potentially help me in becoming a new creation in Christ. I didn't even hesitate! That ministry was so fulfilling that we didn't go every two weeks as the Mercy Team did; we went on our own weekly and eventually multiple times a week. It wasn't long until we became a part of 7 Bridges to Recovery. There it is. You never know what can happen until you respond to an opportunity that God sets before you. But I must ask, have you even been looking for opportunities? You never know what it is that God may want you to get involved in if you don't open your eyes and ears. Something as small and routine we do today could be something that God wants you to be seriously involved with later. It all comes down to what you are willing to do.

God wants to make you a new man if you let Him. I believe we need to put all our focus on Him and not what's going on in the world. That junk can do nothing for us. I've been involved in men's ministry for some time now and I have witnessed so many men wanting to hold on to their current selves. It just won't work. God can't use you if you are living your old life. Your old self can only be used as a testimony to God's greatness in transforming you. God is so specific that He might even want to change your physical appearance as well. I believe it's very possible in order for God to use you for a specific task, He knows how He wants you to be as well as what He might want you to look like. A lot of the time men don't hear any of that because they are too busy trying to look like how they want to. Instead of doing that, we need to ask God what he thinks.

Let me explain it to you this way. When I first started going to church I used to look pretty hardcore. I was 250 lbs., I wore Harley Davidson clothing, harness boots, and a gold loop earring. This was my bouncer-look. As God began to work, and I became more submissive to Him, I began to change. As I began to change internally, I began to change externally as well. I'm not saying wearing these things are wrong, but I believe it is important that we are careful what image we portray. People are supposed to see Jesus in us. We need to look and act like Christ.

So, as I said, I began to work on my image, and this was not by my choice. I followed what I believe God was impressing upon me. It went as far as the Holy Spirit having me get rid of my earring. I am serious. I remember this particular Sunday, I was getting ready for church and I knew that I was supposed to take out my loop. I ignored the prompting. The following week the same thing happened, only this time I took it out and left it out. A few months later I put my loop back in and right away I felt like I was being watched and I felt my body getting very hot. I immediately removed the earring never to put it back in again. Now, I'm sharing this so you can give God a chance to show you what He wants to change in you, internally and externally. You have to understand that it's not about the image that you are trying to create; it's about the image that God wants to create.

If you are military, we know that you are military because of the military image that you have; namely the way your hair is cut as well as the uniform, but also the way you carry yourself. Years after I got out of the Army, people would still ask me if I was military. They would say, "Yeah, I could tell."

Later on I created an image that said "Stay away." It was my demeanor, the way I carried myself, the way I looked, and my size. As men, we create images to show people who we are and what we stand for. God wants the same thing for us, but on His terms. Don't worry about this though. If you are serious about surrendering to Him and truly seeking a relationship, God will work out the details. He will change what He thinks is necessary for you to change.

Later on in life, what I learned was that I needed to find my identity in Christ and not in my muscles, or the way I dressed, or what position I held. Our identities are not found in "stuff". Does that make sense? You don't find yourself in the "boy toys" that you have. I know with me, God needed to strip me of all those things because I allowed those things to display who I wanted you to think I was. Today, I know who I am in Christ. I am cautious as to the image I am portraying to others. My facial expressions are not as intimidating as they once were. I don't like showing off the tattoo on my arm because I'm not supposed to draw unwanted attention to myself. People are supposed to be drawn to me because of Jesus inside me. Isn't the goal of being a Christian to be Christ like?

"Do not conform to the pattern of this world, but be transformed by the renewing of your mind. Then you will be able to test and approve what God's will is—his good, pleasing and perfect will."
(Romans 12:2)

"Do not love the world or anything in the world. If anyone loves the world, love for the Father is not in them. For everything in the world— the lust of the flesh, the lust of the eyes, and the pride of life—comes

not from the Father but from the world. The world and its desires pass away, but whoever does the will of God lives forever." (1 John 2:15-17)

Two very powerful scriptures. I believe one of the reasons why men avoid changing their lifestyles to become new is because the desires of the flesh are so strong. It says clearly that we are not to love anything in the world, but yet we have Christ followers debate whether or not tattoos are okay, for example. Is that something the world is participating in? If yes, then why is it so hard to separate ourselves from getting them? Think about it, if you have to question it, a part of you already knows that it's probably wrong or something that God would not approve of.

It doesn't have to be tattoos; it can be anything that the world divulges themselves in. Anything that can be a distraction and doesn't line up with His word. New means for you to become different from the world. You were already doing worldly stuff before you came to know Christ, so that stuff is old. In order to become more like Christ, we have to separate ourselves from worldly things. Jesus associated Himself with all kinds of people, He didn't do what any of them were doing. He was Himself, an image of God and He was humble and modest. When people saw Him coming they knew Him by His presence alone.

New takes time. I definitely understand that. I had so much of the world embedded in my spirit that I had to come to a place of complete brokenness in order for God to do a true work in me. Some of you were or are on the same page. All God wants to do is start the drawing all over again with a clean sheet of paper. You see, the old piece of paper had too many mess ups, too many eraser marks that in some areas the paper had torn. God says He wants to keep the idea of the same drawing, but it's got to be done on a clean sheet of paper. No more eraser marks now when you mess up because you've been forgiven. If we let Him, God will be able to finish the drawing with amazing results. The results that He can accomplish are beyond anything you can ever imagine. If you can change your mindset and just give everything, and I mean everything, over to Him, even the things that seem so insignificant, He will reconstruct your life. You will begin to see a new side of you! A literal new you! Are you ready for that clean sheet of paper?

MY PRAYER: Heavenly Father, I come before You today Lord, to acknowledge You as the potter and we are Your clay. You are the Creator of the Heavens and the Earth. You are *our* Creator. You made us on purpose and for a purpose. I ask You, Lord, work in us so that we may be able to walk in our purpose. I ask You to make us new. I want us to be new creations in Christ and I understand that we need to first surrender ourselves to You completely. My prayer, from today forward is that we lay all of our self at Your feet and say have Your way. We say, "More of You and less of me." Forgive me and the men reading this for doing our own thing. I have to believe that You have tried to speak to us in various ways and we chose to ignore those promptings. I realize that we can no longer live that way. Please, God, show us today, right now how we need to proceed and we will follow. Thank You for Your forgiveness, love, mercy, and grace.

In Jesus name, AMEN!

CHAPTER 15

OBEDIENCE O

"Jesus replied, 'Anyone who loves me will obey my teaching."
(John 14:23).

"But if you look carefully into the perfect law that sets you free, and if you *do what it says* and don't forget what you heard, then God will bless you for doing it." (James 1:25 NLT)

Why do we demand obedience from others, but when it comes to our own obedience we get offended, lazy, or have excuses? Do you think it's because we are adults and we have the right to not answer to anyone? Some of you reading this think exactly that. With you it's "Do as I say, not as I do", right? That's lame. That is an old way of thinking.

Is obedience an easy thing? For some yes, but for many of us, not so much. Part of the reason for this can be found in chapter 14 of this book. Yes, that's right "maturity". Obedience for me was very difficult,

141

especially since I had been out on my own since I was 17. My whole childhood had been about obedience and suffering the wrath of disobedience. Some people who were raised similar to the way I was, seem to have done things differently that I did. Some of them became submissive types. They submitted to anyone who raised their voice an octave higher than their own, which resulted in other issues.

My point is this: for some, obedience would come a little easier once the benefits of being obedient to God are realized. But, for a lot of us, we became defiant to just about all authority figures and we could've cared less about the benefits of obedience. "We're the ones in charge!" We would say. "No one was going to push us down ever again." Anyone know what I'm talking about?

I lived this way for so long; well into my late thirties! It was easy for our type to demand obedience, but when it came time for us to be obedient to someone higher than ourselves, yeah right, that wasn't happening. Most of the stories or testimonies I have shared with you so far required obedience from me in order for God to initiate change. One of the biggest things I had to do at one point was marry Carrie. I married her out of complete obedience. By then, I understood the phrase, "When God speaks, you listen," a little better. So, I listened.

What came as a result of my obedience is something so awesome! God had already shown me so many "marvelous things" just as He promised! **One of the most important things God showed me out**

of obedience is love. I love Carrie more than myself and I receive not only her love in return, but God's love as well. That is a pretty marvelous trade-off, if you ask me.

Another time was when I was told one Saturday morning that I needed to throw away my cigarettes and ashtrays for good. I had been praying for a while on this issue, but nothing ever happened. I mean Carrie and I were in leadership at the church and we snuck around like teenagers smoking; it was very frustrating living like this. If anyone of you has ever attempted to quit smoking you know how hard it is. This particular Saturday morning, Carrie and I were sleeping in a little later, when she wanted to get up and have a cigarette. I asked her not to since it had been awhile since our last cigarette. She wanted a cigarette and that's when I told her that I believe God wants us to quit. She told me that God hadn't told her anything like that, and I have to admit, things got a little out of hand.

I took all the cigarettes and crumpled them up and flushed them down the toilet. That was in August 2008. I haven't touched a cigarette since that day. Carrie quit a week later. She was very upset the way I tried to force her, but God did deal with her in the way He knew would work. I meant well, but it didn't come across too well for her. Out of radical obedience, God helped me to give up a very hard habit, cold turkey.

Obedience requires us to get out of our comfort zone and just trust Him.

I could go into so many more examples where God has shown Himself mighty because of my obedience. I know that many of you have amazing testimonies as well. Do you share them with other men so that they may see and begin to understand the benefits of obedience? Let's look at the scripture out of John 14:15 again. Jesus is speaking here

.

"If you love me, you will obey my teaching."

Do you get that? If you "love" God then you will automatically obey Him. It took me awhile to understand that concept. I mean we think of obedience as a "must do or else" type thing, right? Well, if you read the Old Testament that's pretty much how it was. I mean people were dying for disobeying laws and ordinances, like on the spot. If it were like that today, not a single one of us would be alive. Earth would be barren. I'm so glad God came up with another plan to save us all.

Just yesterday, March 5th, 2015, we celebrated Jesus' resurrection. Yes, Jesus died for each and every one of us because we are all disobedient. The goal, I believe is to become more obedient. Not defiant, but obedient. If we are all sinfully disobedient and Jesus' death covered our sins, what is the point of being obedient? I'm going to give you the simple answer. Love. Yes we are covered by Jesus' blood, but here's the thing. If you say you love Jesus, then everything in you will want to be obedient because you love Him. How you perceive and go about your disobedience, love for Him will change all of that! We might not be able to ever "do" enough, but we can always "love" and be satisfied. This action of love pleases Him and He can trust you more because everything you do is out of obedience to Him.

If you look closely at what I wrote, you will see that obedience comes from love and love comes out of obedience. This type of obedience, I believe comes in time. There is the other type of obedience that plays an integral part in our walk as Christ followers. That's the "just do it" obedience. That's the obedience that takes maturity to do. You do it because it's something you have to do. This is how I started off in my journey. I had to get myself to a point where I just obeyed. I know there were times I didn't even know why; I just obeyed because I knew I had to. As time went on, I began to see different things a little clearer. Every time I obeyed, God showed me something even more awesome than the last time.

Allow me to share a story of when the Holy Spirit guided me and my obedience. Carrie and I had recently picked up another four-legged family member, while Carrie already had her brindle pug, which we have had now for about 5 years. She knew I had been wanting my own dog again for quite some time so I started looking. I eventually came across this cute Australian Shepherd mixed with Pit bull. He was adorable; so adorable, we went ahead and brought him home.

Now, I have had several dogs through the years, and most of them have started with us as puppies. Maxx, this new addition of ours, was only two months old when we picked him up. I had forgotten just how ornery puppies are. Of course they lack any kind of obedience and are just all over the place doing whatever they please. Remember all those times you ran around the house, looking crazy, saying "No", "Stop it", "Put that down"?

Imagine how the puppy must have felt. Everything he did, he heard a voice of correction. Perhaps when you first became a Christ follower, you felt just like the puppy? Didn't it seem like everything you did God was right there telling you, "No". I believe that was your break in period. Not to compare men with dogs, but just like dogs, mankind can be so full of disobedience. Think about it. We are so used to doing whatever we want. Thankfully God had to begin to break that off of us by telling us, "No". It was that way for me anyway.

As Maxx began to mature it seems like I didn't have to say "No" as much. Either he has learned right from wrong and disobedience is out of his system or he's completely done with hearing me yell so many times. Either way, he is learning obedience. I was learning to be more obedient as well. At the time, I might not have necessarily known why I didn't do something, but it didn't matter. Back then I was still learning to obey too.

As Maxx continues to mature he will become more compliant and obey. Yes, treats are included, but, At least he will begin to understand that there is something good he will receive when he has been obedient. It's the same with us. For me, as I mentioned before, God would reward me in some kind of way. The reward isn't always money or something tangible. It can be something that fills you with satisfaction and joy. Your wife telling you that she is proud of you. Whatever it may be, God does reward us for our obedience.

As I continue maturing, I do feel bad when I disobey. Afterwards I am quick to go to God in prayer, repent, and ask for forgiveness. My disobedience leads me right back to my obedience. Now, because Maxx is potty trained, he knows where he can go and where he should not go. He mostly obeys, but sometimes he disobeys and goes where he isn't supposed to. What do I do when this happens? Our dog gets corrected, loved on, and then we move on. God does the same with us. He forgives us, corrects us where necessary, loves us unconditionally, and moves on. He doesn't hold anything against you. Over time, it gets to a point where obeying God becomes second nature. It's something you want to do because you love Him. You submit and serve your wife because you love her, right? I believe, as I mature, I don't hear the "no's" as much because I am more mature. I believe I understand obedience now.

At all costs I will do my best to be obedient to God. My love for Him has gotten so much stronger than what it was before. I'm not saying that God doesn't tell me no. What I am saying is that He can trust me with the things I come to Him in prayer for. I know what His Word says and therefore I obey. As men, the more obedient we become, the more it is implanted in us. Of course, anytime I fall short and sin, I go to Him and repent. I seek His forgiveness daily.

There is a difference between being defiant, disobedient on purpose, and disobeying on accident. What I mean with disobeying on accident is the fact that you are not living in the lifestyle of disobeying God. When your lifestyle is consumed with continuous sin just because you want to, that's being defiant. But when you are striving every day to live upright and stay in His will, but you sin, that is still disobeying Him. Living in obedience doesn't mean you have become perfect. It means when you do mess up, you seek His forgiveness and repent. God is with us like we are with our kids. They disobey us quite often, but we don't kick them to the curb, right? We still love them and we reward them when they are good, right? Where do you think we get that level of love from? We get it from our heavenly Father. If we can be that way towards our children, just think how much more God can do for you and me.

Obedience does not have to be some mundane task; it can be looked as worship. Have you ever thought of it that way? I promise you, I surely did not see obedience as any kind of worship. Regardless of my thoughts, it is though. If we are obedient through our reverence to Him, He receives it as praise and worship. You might be in a place right now where you don't see obedience as anything good and more like a pain in the rear. And I get it; I too was there. I know a whole lot of men reading this have been there. This is where endurance and perseverance come in, chapter 5. If you can make yourself get out of bed at 5 am to go running every morning, you will soon see the benefits and then you won't have to force yourself out of bed, you'll get up gladly. You get my point?

Obedience will become second nature to you if you just keep pressing through. It's the same with any other topic I am writing about. Don't beat yourself up when you disobey, simply go and pray, seek God's forgiveness, receive His love that is unconditional, and keep it moving. Obedience does not have to be some kind of burden or thing that you feel you *have* to do. It's real simple if you think about it. If you love God, then you'll do. No one has to make you do anything; you'll do it because you love Him.

I have learned out of my own experiences that obedience comes in levels, depending on where I am with Christ. If we can only receive what our maturity allows us to receive, then so it is with obedience as well. We all have to start somewhere. James 1:22 says, "Don't just listen to God's Word, you must do what it says." You **must** do what it says or else you will deceive yourself. We read the words, but we don't automatically do just because the words on the page tell us to, right? There is more to it than that which will compel us to "do" something. Whether you are at the start of your journey or if you are in the middle of your journey and still struggle with being obedient, ask yourself this: "What is it going to take to compel me to obey? I believe for me, it was just the fact that I wanted to change. I was sick and tired of being sick and tired. I was willing to try anything that God was going to throw my way.

Like I said earlier on in this chapter, I had to get myself to a place of just being obedient regardless of how I felt or what I thought. I wasn't very good at it at first, but it got easier. And like I said, now I am at a point where I obey out of love, not with the feeling of "I have to". But guess what? I don't have to. God has given me that choice. But I do have to because I love God. My love for God gives me no other choice but to obey. If I didn't love God then yeah, I wouldn't have to, it's my choice. It's your choice as well. It's either you love Him or you don't. There's no gray area here. Take a look at this eye opener:

"We know that we have come to know him if we keep his commands. Whoever says, "I know him," but does not do what he commands is a liar, and the truth is not in that person. But if anyone obeys his word, love for God is truly made complete in them. This is how we know we are in him: Whoever claims to live in him must live as Jesus did."
(1 John 2:3-6)

I could have opened this chapter with that verse, but I decided to use it here at the closing. A little bit more to think about. God is telling us that if we claim to know God and we don't do what He commands us to do in His Word, we are liars because there can be no truth in us. Again, no gray area here. Either you love God as you claim you do and obey Him or you don't and He considers you a liar. This goes along with Jesus speaking this scripture below:

"So, because you are lukewarm—neither hot nor cold—I am about to spit you out of my mouth." (Revelation 3:16)

This actually applies to everything and anything. If our walk with God is going to be lukewarm as the scripture says, then why even bother? He says it right here that He will spit you out of His mouth. I say wherever you are right now in your walk; ask God what He says about your obedience. Is He pleased with it or is it lacking? Are you still acting like an 18-year-old rebel at 40? The only way you will ever have a mature relationship with your Creator is through obedience. God sees obedience as being better than sacrifice, as an act of faith, as praise and worship, and most of all it proves that we love Him. With all that said, God never forgets those who are obedient to Him, He blesses us beyond what we could ever imagine! We don't learn obedience overnight; it's a lifelong process that we pursue by making it a daily goal.

"Because we have these promises, dear friends, let us cleanse ourselves from everything that can defile our body or spirit. And let us work toward complete holiness because we fear God."
(2 Corinthians 7:1)

MY PRAYER: Heavenly Father, as we have just finished up discussing obedience, my prayer for those who are reading this book as well as for all men, is that we really seek You, Lord. We need to understand this life-long change process. To understand what it really means to be obedient to You and to Your commands. Lord, we have been programmed to be self-sufficient and make decisions on our own. Please renew our minds and lift that off of us men, in the name of Jesus. May we come to surrender ourselves to You out of obedience. Lord, there are many who haven't come to the point of obeying You as second nature; please help them and soften their hearts so they can receive from You the tools necessary to obey You. Lord, we are all sinners. Forgive us as we come to You humbly and repent. Thank You for washing us clean. Thank You for clearing the slate of our disobedience. I pray that we would love You so much as to obey You without thinking twice about it. May we obey You, God our Creator, as an act of faith. Let our obedience be an act better than sacrifice. Let it be as praise and worship to You; but most of all, out of love for You. I personally thank You, Father, for allowing me to participate in this wonderful act of worship; writing this book. So many men will read this book and come to know You. Your grace has empowered each man to become the man that You intended him to be. A man created on purpose, for a purpose.

Thank You, Lord!

In Jesus' name, AMEN!

CHAPTER 16

PURPOSE

P

"For I know the plans I have for you," declares the Lord, "plans to prosper you and not to harm you, plans to give you hope and a future. Then you will call on me and come and pray to me, and I will listen to you. You will seek me and find me when you seek me with all your heart." (Jeremiah 29:11-13)

I've read a commentary or two where the writer claims the verses of this chapter doesn't apply in the way that we like to use them. That's fine, if that's what you want to believe. I know for myself, these verses speak to me in such a tremendous way. I can't believe any other way that it wasn't meant for me to receive. This scripture is one of the very first I memorized. I love believing that God has a plan and purpose for me. What about you? Do you read this scripture and keep on moving, not giving it much thought? If you do, let me ask you why? Why would you ignore one of God's promises?

Since we are discussing purpose, allow me to further tell you about this ministry, Man On Purpose and how it all came about. Jeremiah 29:11 is in the logo as it is the driving verse of the whole ministry. The tagline says it all: Become the man you are intended to be with purpose, on purpose. That's right! You and I were created on purpose with a purpose! When I finally learned that, my whole life really started to change. I struggled with the "why am I here?" question for some time, perhaps like many of you. Even during the beginning years of being a Christ follower I tried so many things on my own to figure out the answer to that question.

I remember getting involved in various ministries thinking that might be what I was supposed to do. While the ministries were very fulfilling, I still felt as though something was always missing. Something bigger. I recall a time where Carrie and I were so involved in the homeless ministry that we thought we were supposed to start our own shelter for the homeless. We even found a similar hotel property as where we met and lived in 2002. We thought out loud, "Hey! We could turn this property into a homeless shelter community." I actually researched the property and found the owner. Carrie and I used to go to the property and pray over it every week for a few months. But as the story goes, God never opened that door for us and we never started that homeless shelter.

During a two year span we looked for and found other properties that we thought could work for a homeless shelter. Nothing ever came of it for us. This went from 2006 to about 2009. In March of 2008 another ministry opportunity came along. This ministry was a Christian 12 step program called Celebrate Recovery. I won't go into the details, but Carrie and I were chosen as the ministry leaders. Carrie was over the women and I was co-leader over the men. It was an awesome experience and I received so much healing myself. I was involved in Celebrate Recovery for about 2 years.

From about 2007 to October 2012, I was also one of the leads on the church's security team, which I really liked doing as well. All the while I still couldn't figure out just what my purpose was. I knew it was more than just a paycheck from my job, which was in the hotel industry as a Chief Engineer, which was also a leadership role.

I had started and ran various businesses through the years as well. Everything from landscaping, contractor, auto detailing, graphic design, T-shirt design all the way to starting a Harley Davidson accessories manufacturing company. For years I had no idea what I was put on earth for, and it seemed like I would never find out. On December 17, 2010, I lost yet another job. I had been in the hotel industry for eight years at this point and I worked my way up to multi property Director of Engineer in one of the leading hotel corporations. I hadn't a clue what God was about to do in my life. In August of 2011, I was blessed with the opportunity to be trained and certified by John C. Maxwell. So, on February 18, 2012, I received my certificate as a Certified Teacher, Coach, and Speaker with the John Maxwell Company in Palm Beach Gardens, Florida at a 3-day conference.

When I returned home I thought I was to continue with MasterMind groups, teaching the John Maxwell topics and so I facilitated a group in "Everyone Communicates, Few Connect". Prior to this I facilitated "The 21 Irrefutable Laws of Leadership". I soon came to find that God had a different plan for me. On Saturday April 18, 2012, at about 9:00 a.m. I woke up to the Holy Spirit speaking to me. I got up and grabbed my iPad and began writing down what I felt He was impressing upon me.

One thing I am sure of is this: Man on Purpose was to be about empowering men to become the men they are intended to be with purpose, on purpose. I was also told to put together a men's event. *Yikes*, I thought. But I obeyed God's voice regardless of the unknown. On August 04, 2012, I held my first men's event at World Outreach Church for all Nations in Lawrenceville, Georgia.

I taught from John Maxwell's book, *The 15 Laws of Personal Growth*. This was given to us in note form at the John Maxwell Team Conference in February. By the time this book was released on October 2, 2012, it title changed to *The 15 Laws of Invaluable Growth*. After the event, the pastor who helped us hold the event at his church went up to Carrie and told her that if I ever tried to do anything else besides speaking and teaching at men's events, to contact him so that he could set me straight. I guess he believed that I was operating in my calling, or my purpose.

As you can see, all the years of ministry work, serving, leadership training, and even some of the businesses were all necessary to get me to my purpose. I believe God leaves nothing to waste; He can use everything in your life. Where are you now with your purpose? Have you figured out what your purpose is? Take a look back and add everything up that you have ever been involved with. Is it possible that God has been trying to make you aware of your purpose and you have missed His promptings? Have others mentioned something to you that you may have just shrugged off?

You are important and God has an important purpose for you. Your purpose is one of the greatest reasons why I am writing this book. I want to help men see how important finding their purpose in this life is. I want to show men how useful they can really be for building God's kingdom, instead of their own.

"And we know that in all things God works for the good of those who love him, who have been called according to his purpose."
(Romans 8:28)

If you let God guide you in the direction of your purpose, He can and will work out all the things that you encounter along the way. He always has your best interest at heart. God did not create you and me to do whatever we want to do. He created us for His purpose. When we are functioning in our purpose, which is God's will for us, that's when we are complete.

"For we are God's handiwork, created in Christ Jesus to do good works, which God prepared in advance for us to do."
(Ephesians 2:10)

Here's the thing about your purpose. The purpose that God has for you does not necessarily mean that it's something that you are good at, or something you like to do. If you paid attention at all, when I first began serving in ministry, it wasn't something I was very thrilled about doing. I had to learn to love the last, the least, and the lost in the streets of Atlanta. As I stepped out into doing something, that's when God showed up and began working in me to soften my heart towards these individuals. Everything kind of just fell into place from there. I believe learning and growing in Christianity enables us to get better at hearing from God. The more we give of ourselves to Him, the more we get better at hearing Him. It is at this moment that God can begin to use you. It's through that process that you'll discover your purpose in life. Take a look at a few pointers: Working with God to find your life purpose means working as a team. When you take a step, God takes two.

Be willing to try some things that interest you.

You will know very quickly if you've found the right thing for you. Doors will either open or slam shut. Either way, you'll know where you stand. Like I mentioned before, for me it all started with stepping out into the homeless ministry. What will you step out into?

Be Patient.

Wanting to know everything *right this second* is pretty common these days. Learning to trust that God will show you when He's ready—but that takes patience. God isn't going to show you every piece of the puzzle all at once. If He did, you'd get that "deer in the headlights" look, because you'd be so overwhelmed by it all. Not to mention you'd be overly tempted to come up with a back-up plan "just in case" things didn't work out. There's no way I would have been able to take it all in at once. I mean if God had told me back then everything I have been able to do over the last few years, I probably would have ran or something. It has been an accumulation of time to fill the shoes that God had for me to fit into.

Don't waste your time on things you know aren't from God.

"Get rich quick" schemes never work. Finding a Christian husband or wife won't happen if you're focused on activities and events that don't involve Christians. And let me include participating in things you know are wrong—well, you're simply prolonging your answers. I surely have been guilty of this. Just ask Carrie how many "other" endeavors I got myself into. As a matter of fact, just a few days before I fasted and the Holy Spirit impressed upon me to write this book, I was getting ready to manufacture a product that I spent money on designing and prototyping. This was not the first time. I know that Man On Purpose is my ministry, but I'm kind of stubborn, I guess.

Don't let the people around you talk you into things.

Just because it sounds like a good idea from the world, doesn't mean it's God's plan for you. Following God's leading sometimes means you have to say "No" to many well-meaning family members or friends. It comes down to the decision to follow God, no matter where He leads. Carrie has always wanted for me to do what God was calling me to do. That's one good thing. Since then, I haven't had anyone try and talk me into other things.

Lastly, don't ever give up.

You may not know your specific purpose today or tomorrow, but as long as you're really great at being a Christian, and your heart is open, you **will** find God and He **will** find you. I'm still learning how to be a great Christian, but I do what I can and let God do the rest. I actually did give up a couple of times. I let Satan talk me out of my own purpose. I got to a point where I would question myself, *Who do you think you are trying to pour into other men's life when you need advice, just as much, if not more?* But then I found out that God doesn't call the qualified, He qualifies the called. Anyone that God calls for His purpose, He provides what is needed along the way and during.

"That is why, for Christ's sake, I delight in weaknesses, in insults, in hardships, in persecutions, in difficulties. For when I am weak, then I am strong." (2 Corinthians 12:10)

Although I did briefly give up a couple of times, I was always led back. Once you know your purpose, you can't move on without it. So, from experience I say to you: "DON'T GIVE UP"

(Karen Wolff, a contributing writer for About.com)

Men, I don't know what each of your purposes are, but I hope this chapter and this book can help you navigate a little better. I believe for men everywhere, one very important purpose is your servanthood in the community, church, and ministry. Far too many of you think that "bringing home the bacon" from your careers is all you need to do. God did not create you for these reasons only.

Take a look around your churches and see what's going on. I would take a poke and say that maybe 4 out of 10 men are serving in the church at any capacity. Men built and led the church in the Bible. I am urging men to really get serious and stop waiting for your purpose to fall from the sky. Get involved. Do something and let God direct your steps. You will never be completely fulfilled deep within without knowing and operating in your purpose. The same passion that you put into your sports, recreation, and big boy toys should be directed more towards God. Greater rewards await you.

MY PRAYER:

Heavenly Father, I believe Lord that it's Your will for every man to seek and walk in their purpose; the purpose that You created them for. My prayer is that every man would seek You to find their purpose. So many men are living unfulfilled lives due to the fact they have no clue why they even exist. God, You know that I felt that way for a very long time until You made it clear to me what my purpose was. I thank You for that and again I pray and wish the same for every man. Lord, right now as I am praying this prayer, You have so many men specifically that need to receive this message and this prayer. I pray they receive both, in the name of Jesus. Lord, You are the Creator and You know why You made each and every one of us. All we have to do is step out in faith and receive. Teach us Lord to become humble men just like Christ was when He walked the earth. We want to testify and glorify Your name and Your Word. I pray for men all across this world to rise up and stand firm and lead in such a powerful way that the world can't help but to take notice and respond to You. Forgive us for our "lukewarm" behaviors. Turn up the temperature in our heart so that we may become "hot" for You. It is Your great works that we desire to do throughout this land, not ours. Lord, may Your will be done in each and every one of our lives, so that You may receive all the glory!

In Jesus' name, AMEN!

CHAPTER (17)

QUIET (Q)

"Be still before the Lord and wait patiently for him; do not fret when people succeed in their ways, when they carry out their wicked schemes." (Psalm 37:7)

Noise, noise; everywhere noise! What a noisy world we live in. I don't know about you, but I love peace and quiet. I seek peace and quiet every chance I can. I get a lot of it because I make it for myself. This verse from Psalm tells us to "Be still before the Lord". Have you forgotten what it means to be still or quiet? I mean, if and when you had young kids, you'd tell them all the time to be quiet, right? Ok, granted, some of you might not have any kids at all, but I am sure you've told someone to be quiet at some point in your life.

In this chapter, being quiet and being still go hand in hand. With this chapter I want to take a look at the importance of making quiet time before God. You might be thinking that it's the same as praying. Yes, it can be, but it doesn't necessarily have to be. Follow along and let's see if

I can explain what I believe God wants me to write.

I saw this quote somewhere: "Prayer is when you talk to God, Meditation is when you listen." I'm not going to call it "meditation" here, it sounds a bit too Zen? I want it to be called what it is, quiet or quiet time. Same difference, I know. Have you ever heard of "noise junkies"? Neither had I until just now. These are people just like "food junkies" except they can't live without noise or better yet, music. I think this is a made up word because there is no scientific evidence that these people even exist, but I'm sure you know some people however that just love noise. No, I'm not talking about the 3-year-old running around banging on his toys, although they are included. Maybe you are a bit of a "noise junkie" and you don't even know it? Let's see.

I believe a "noise junkie" to be a person, like I mentioned in the previous paragraph that just can't seem to be without some kind of noise in their life. They wake up and the first thing they do is turn on the TV. Actually, each room they go into they turn on something, maybe a phone app or even the radio. They leave the house and get into their car, but from the house they have earphones in their ears. Once they get into the car, the earphones come out and the radio gets turned on. They get to work and their earphones get popped back in until they reach their office or cubicle. At that point the radio gets turned on again. I could keep on going, but I hope you get my point. You might say, "Maybe they just like music." Yeah, maybe that is true. Or maybe they are just trying to drown out anything from coming in?

These individuals never give anyone or anything a chance to come in. Why do you think the teenagers have earphones glued to their head? They don't want to hear parents yapping at them. I definitely don't think it's a good idea to let our kids walk around with earphones attached to their heads. The biggest reason is because they turn out to be the adults that we are talking about right now. They have no concept at all what the word "quiet" means. How can they receive anything from anyone with foam and rubber glued to their ears? What goes in must come out. What goes up must come down. See the law at work here?

I am talking about filling our minds with so much junk that we can't hear God's instructions! Just like our bodies need to be flushed of toxins, so does our minds. How do we flush our minds of the junk that we keep putting in them? It's real simple, and you don't even have to drink anything that tastes nasty. Ok, how then? How about this: TURN STUFF OFF! It's simply pushing a button that says: OFF. No way. Yes way!

For some of you, this is a new concept. There is a second part to the brain detox and that is to just sit. After you've turned everything off, then just sit and let your brain voice a huge, "THANK YOU!"

Some of you are like, "Are you kidding me"? "Is this guy for real"? If you don't believe me, the next time you are gathered around your co-workers just listen to what they talk about. Any time you are in a group of people, listen to what they are saying. Most times they are talking about some crap that happened on this or that show. Nothing of importance at all.

You see, people talk about what they know. If all they do is watch TV and listen to talk radio, then that's all they know to talk about. If a person is filling themselves with God's Word and decent wholesome shows and movies, then that's what they talk about. Look what happens around each sport season. Who scored what touchdown? Who fouled who? What plays do you think should have happened? Etc. That's what a lot of guys you know talk about. Am I right? I know I'm right because I hear it all the time, and so do you. It is as if sports have taken over their lives. Then they wonder why they can't hear from God when they need Him most. Some of you can't even put the remote down long enough to say a complete prayer. You can't wait to get out of church so your sports day can begin. It's pretty sad actually.

It doesn't have to be just you sports, guys. What about movie fanatics, gym fanatics, or you "grown up kids" playing video games all the time? Anything other than God that possesses most of your time is an idol. I know that God wants us to give at least 10% of our income as tithe, but I haven't read anywhere where it says to give only 10% of ourselves. He wants you and me 100%.

One of the main reasons is exactly what we are discussing here in this chapter. If there's more of Him in our lives, then there's more fruit. If you plant seeds and tend to them only a small percentage of the time, chances are you'll get a pretty crappy crop. It's no difference in us. In order to reach our full potential in Him, we have to be cultivated. One of the ways God cultivates us is with "being quiet", or as the scripture says to "be still".

I know that I have the tendency to come across as being a little harsh and judgmental, but let me remind you, I'm the last person that would ever judge any of you. Now if you see me as being a little harsh it's only because I have a deep passion to see the best that God has in store for all of us.

Look, I am compassionate because I, too, have issues

still. This is not just for you; it's for me as well. I just want us as men to be on fire for God and put Him first in our lives. I know that God has a better purpose for each and every one of you guys. Satan is a liar and a thief. He comes to steal, kill, and destroy. If he can keep you busy with extracurricular activities and keep your focus off God, then that's exactly what he will do. I'm not saying that the "other stuff" that you participate in is wrong. What I am saying however is for you to stop, and take a long, hard look at the "other stuff" and see for yourself if they are taking up too much of your time.

Be still and reflect. That's what quiet is all about. All these other things that you participate in, I call noise. It doesn't matter if it's the sports' stuff, movies, hunting, cars, motorcycles, or even work; it can all look and sound like a bunch of noise. Some noises are louder than others, and a lot of the time these loud noises are the ones that deafen us to hearing the smaller, quieter noises.

Have any of you ever just took some time and sat somewhere far away from all the noise? I mean, just sat there and did absolutely nothing? I do quite often, and it is so refreshing. You don't even have to go anywhere special, just wait until everyone is gone for the day and it's just you and the Lord in the house or apartment. There are a few rules, though. #1) Don't turn on anything at all. Feel free to have your water, coffee or juice, but that's it. #2) Then go sit in your favorite chair. Sit there and see what happens. Quiet! Again, at this point I'm not talking about praying or anything. Oh, #3) I forgot to mention that electronics have to be turned off. Our cell phones and gadgets can be a huge hindrance.

I mentioned earlier in this book that I purposely took 3 days off to fast and to begin writing this book. Well, during this time I wrote the first 7 chapters! I've had other times where I was just sitting and listening to God when He would impress upon me things that I need to do for Him, someone else, or myself. At first I would question whether it was really Him telling me these things, but the only way to truly know at first was to just act on it, you'll find out soon enough if it was just you or if it was something God impressed upon you.

One of the problems I have seen through the years is that men won't act upon what they know they should do. I can't tell you how many times I've heard men say that they should have done this or that, but they just weren't sure about it. Then I would ask them if they ran it by anyone else and most of the time the answer was no. So, they shortchanged themselves, why? Pride, embarrassment, or they just didn't want to believe that God could use them for that particular situation? So then the cycle continues. Men stop listening, because they don't _____. You fill in the blank with your own excuse. You notice I said excuse instead of reason? Because that's what it is, an excuse.

Come on guys, please! It's better to try and be wrong, than to have never tried at all. God knows how many times I have been wrong! If you don't believe me, then call Carrie. She will tell you. What I've learned is this: it's the heart that matters to God. Accuracy comes with time. The other thing I've learned about my quiet times is that sometimes God will impress something upon us that won't happen until sometime later on. But we won't know that until we move forward by choosing and then doing.

A lot of these action themes have been covered in previous chapters. I just want to encourage you to commit and try it on for size. See how being still fits you. A lot of things we are discussing in this book, for example, are things that some of you are going to have to force yourself to do. It may take a while before a lot of this becomes second nature. This topic is no different. You are going to have to do it because it's something that is necessary to do, bottom line. You need to let God work out the rest.

Ironically, being still or quiet isn't something that I am unfamiliar with. You see, as a child I spent countless days in "punishment" in my room, just sitting there. Let's not forget the living room, or wherever else they would have me. Many times I just stood in the corner for hours and hours. Of course, as an adult I needed a lot of "noise" in my life because I thought quiet was a not so good thing. Childhood experiences will do that to you, but thankfully it was my wonderful God who would show me just how good and beneficial quiet time was and still is. So, now I challenge you to give it a try.

MY PRAYER:

Heavenly Father, yet another chapter has been completed for Your glory, Lord. I pray everything that has been written does exactly what You want it to do. I pray that those who read this will have a better understanding of how important being "quiet" really is to You, but also how important it is for them. Thank You, Lord for Your teachings. Give us all the opportunity to share them with others. I pray that You will be with those who struggle with this topic or any of the topics in this book. Guide them to Your promises. I pray strong men would come alongside those who are struggling and raise them up and mentor them. Heavenly Father, may men receive Your instructions, directions, and their purpose during their quiet time with You. I pray that men would have ears to hear, and that their hearts would be softened to receive all that You have for them. I pray for a fresh renewing of what quiet time is and what it means for those who already practice this. And for those who don't quite know or understand what it is, I pray that they will have their eyes opened. May we learn not to just slow down, but to be intentional and make time to be quiet. We want to hear Your voice in the midst of this noisy world.

In Jesus' name, AMEN!

CHAPTER 18
RECEIVE
R

"Until now you have not asked for anything in my name. Ask and you will receive, and your joy will be complete." (John 16:24)

We started off this journey in chapter 1 with, ASK and now we have reached this chapter and we see the topic is RECEIVE. The above verse says to "ask and you will receive". That's a true promise, which a lot of you already know. We also learned that a lot of times we don't receive because of what we discussed in chapter 1. "Ask and you shall receive".

The *receive* that I believe I'm supposed to write about in this chapter is something God needs all men to understand. It's more about receiving when you have done nothing to earn what's been given to you. It's this kind of receiving we tend to struggle with the most. You see, we have been taught that we need to *earn* what we get. But if any of you have been a Christ follower for any amount of time now, then you know this is an untrue teaching. Society teaches that in order to have, you need to be in control and go out and get it! God teaches us that He freely gives and all we have to do is ask. That's right. If you have gotten over your issues of chapter 1, then you are well on your way to receiving from Him in accordance to His will for you.

What's up with this kind of receiving? I remember growing up as a child and hearing my father and mother stop us kids all the time from receiving from anyone. For instance, if a neighbor just wanted to give us a quarter for no particular reason, I would have to politely say, "No, thank you." I was never to receive anything that was freely given from anyone. You can only imagine how I struggled with what God's Word says about receiving.

There's a song I want to share the chorus with you here. The artist is Calvin Nowell, so if you can go on the Internet and google: "Receive" by Calvin Nowell. Listen to the words carefully. This song is all about what I hope you will get out of this chapter. Here is the chorus in case you can't listen to the song right now:

> *Lord, I receive your love here in this moment*
> *Your mercy flows like rain on this heart dry and broken*
> *I receive your love today*
> *It's hard to believe - All I must do is receive*
> *Sweet mystery - All I must do is receive*

Isn't it hard to believe that all we have to do is receive? It's easier said than done. I have learned that receiving is not always about me. What I mean is when someone gives, as we discussed in chapter 6, they are doing so to be a blessing and when we don't receive from them we actually are hindering them in receiving *their* blessing. There is good in both. The Bible says that it is better to give than to receive, which is a true statement. But remember in giving, there will always be someone on the receiving end. I believe to become a good receiver; we must first become a great giver. I know for me it was hard to receive anything from anyone because of what I was taught about receiving. It was like receiving from others was a bad thing. I have since learned that it is not a bad thing at all and God showed me this through giving.

I don't want you to get the wrong idea and think I am talking about receiving "things" like money or gifts. This is part of it because God does give gifts, however, I am talking more about receiving from God what He wants you to have. First and foremost God wants you to receive His spirit into your life. What else can you think of that God wants you to receive from Him that you have been reluctant to accept? Think about that for a few minutes.

Here are a few other things that I believe God has given to us that we just need to receive if we haven't already:

 * Freely we have received His grace and mercy, and freely we should extend that same grace and mercy to others.
* Freely we have received His forgiveness of our sins, and freely we should forgive others of their transgressions.
* Freely we have received His encouragement, and freely we should

encourage others.

* Freely we have received His wisdom, and freely we should share that wisdom with others.

* Freely we have received His love, and freely we should show that love to others.

Did you do anything to earn those? I don't think so. God has given those to us freely, no strings attached. All we need to do is receive them. You and I can't do anything to earn what God has freely given to us. You see, everything you have received from this book so far are merely tools to have a better relationship with Him. Each topic is something to prepare us and mature us to receive all that He has in store. My goal is not for you to become the man you are intended to be with purpose, on purpose to "earn" anything. It's all about becoming complete in who you are in Christ.

I was talking with a friend of mine the other day about how we men like to create our own identities. As we get older we tend to want to hide who we really are to fit in with everyone else. The funny thing about that is God has already given us our identity and all we need to do is receive it from Him, not run away from it because a few guys think it's soft or weird. God made me to be a certain way and because of my hurts and disappointments from childhood, I decided I was going to become the protector of myself and create this big tough guy image in order to do that. Hey, guess what? It worked for a while. Until who I was supposed to be started to come alive.

Again, if I knew any better all I needed to do was receive from God my life's plan and things would have been much different. I had to become intentional in receiving alternate plans from God to get me on track with who I am in Christ, not who I created myself to be. Or better yet, who I allowed the world create. Believe it or not, that is actually what you're doing or have done. It's not you or me creating anything. We allow our society to shape and mold us.

God gives us the capabilities of being leaders in His kingdom, not followers in the world. I get it. I mean, I understand why we like to be our "own man", it gives us a sense of worth and value. It's a lie though. You don't find that in creating something the world values. You can only find true worth and value in God and in receiving His plans for your life. I guess you think that it might be better to make your own instead of receiving anything from God, because then there's no obligation. You can be and do whatever you want, whenever you want, without receiving from anyone. You don't *owe* anyone anything, right? Again, that's how Satan wants you to think. It's another lie!

God gives not expecting anything in return. Everything He gives us is to make us better. Not only that, but He gives us things that are really good for us. The things that God wants you to receive are things that you and I are looking for anyway in life, they are just packaged differently. The world has made their package extremely attractive to the eyes on the outside, but once you begin opening it up, it's empty, unfulfilling without truth. God's package may or may not be as appealing, but once you get into His package, what you see is what you get; the real deal. You get the fullness, truth, and the life that is so much more rewarding.

Why would I give up God's gifts, which are free with no strings attached, for temporary, unfulfilling gifts that the world has to offer? The world makes us continually work towards earning those gifts, with deception all around it.

God is the One who has given women the gift of beauty, but you see the world's gift of beauty means to go and chop up their faces and add this or remove that. The world teaches that beauty is on the outside, not on the inside. Again, this is a big lie Satan tells women, and so many of them believe it.

The gifts that God gives come from within; they have depth and meaning. Nothing that the world teaches or shows has any depth; it's all superficial, surface junk that doesn't last.

I wrote a few paragraphs back that God gives to us not expecting anything in return; there is something I need to add to that statement. I believe He does expect us to be good stewards over what He gives us. Think about it, isn't being a good steward over what we've received the least we can do? Take a look at this verse:

"From everyone who has been given much, much will be demanded; and from the one who has been entrusted with much, much more will be asked." (Luke 12:48)

Keep in mind one thing: **what we receive from God is not dependent on anything we do or don't do.** God gives freely because He loves freely. But if God has given you the responsibility of teaching others, then you need to do it towards the utmost of His glory, right? I believe within this verse lies another reason why a lot of men won't receive from God. They won't receive their purpose or calling because of the responsibility that comes with it.

A lot of men, and this might include you, would prefer to skate through life and let the "other guy" pick up the slack. You justify your situation with all kinds of excuses as to why you should be doing exactly what you are doing. If our vision in life isn't clear, our doing makes us feel like we are doing absolutely nothing. If you are doing for yourself; you surely aren't receiving much from God because your eyes aren't fixed on Him. This is where that ugly word pride comes in.

I believe once you have become a Christian, or a Christ follower, it becomes your duty and/or privilege to receive from God. I say duty because in order to grow in your relationship with Him, you have to receive from His source. You can't grow without receiving from Him the things vital to grow. I also say privilege because not once in Scripture does

God say that we "owe" Him. I definitely see that as a privilege, don't you? It is only by His grace that any of us are even still on this earth. God could have wiped us all out long ago similar to when He restarted with Noah and his family, but He made a way for you and me to be redeemed. Through the sacrifice and resurrection of Jesus our Savior, we can be free from sin and the consequences of it. That is great news!

What is hindering you in receiving from God? If you say nothing, then why won't you receive from Him? What are your reasons? Let us be totally honest with ourselves. No shame, no judgment, no condemnation, none of that here. I am asking that you merely be truthful. Plus, it's not like I can see your answer anyway… Only God can. He knows everything, so you aren't really hiding anything at all. He just wants you to be truthful.

The following is one definition I have encountered with several men throughout the years. If that's you, then you can do something about it. If it's not you, then keep on reading. If you know someone who is, then hopefully you'll reach out to them.

- **Someone who is too afraid to do what is right or expected; someone who is not at all brave or courageous**.

Can you guess what word this definition is for? Yes, you know what it is. It's the word COWARD. I use this word not to judge you, but to simply tell you that it is okay. It is okay for you to be afraid, for now anyway. The goal is for you to see your faults so that you can move forward in receiving the help necessary from God.

I too was once a coward. I ran away from everything. I did not want to face my issues either. I was talking with my friend Graham the other day about how it takes strength to expose ourselves. It takes courage and strength to admit our faults. The good news is that none of us has to do any of this alone. As simple as it sounds, all we have to do is receive. It's time for men to stop acting cowardly and let God be your strength where you are weak. I know no matter how physically strong I may be, or how physically tough I may be, or even how mentally tough I am, it's no match for the strength God has for me. That power from God is what breaks down the strongholds.

"The weapons we fight with are not the weapons of the world. On the contrary, they have divine power to demolish strongholds."
(2 Corinthians 10:4)

But we have to allow ourselves to receive that power and strength from God. You and I will never be able to do battle with the enemy in our own strength. The other options are to try and live a life hiding, which is cowardly. We could live a life always running away, which is also cowardly. Or we could simply lift our hands and receive. Cowardly? I don't think so...

The words pride and ignorance comes to mind as well. I only add pride and ignorance to the mix because anytime you have the instructions or user's manual right in front of your face and you still choose to ignore what's in it because you think you know better, it is called only one of two things.

Or for the sake of another scenario, let's say it's not in front of your face. Instead, all you have to do is extend your hand and receive it from Him. But for whatever the reason, you don't. I'm not sure what we should call that? That's a lot of men's situation as well. Regardless the good news is all that can change in an instance! Make a decision to receive from God. It's already there for you. You don't have to stand in line like at the grocery store or something and wait your turn. No, everything is already available to you. It has your name embroidered on it. Whatever it may be is waiting to be given to you specifically. God only wants you to receive it! It's like that UPS package that has been sitting on your porch for however long, and you just keep walking by it. Little do you know, as soon as you open it, everything will change. From that moment, your life will never be the same!

I challenge you today; grab the package, take it to your kitchen counter, grab some scissors, slice it open and pray! Watch what happens when you receive what God has for you. You will never be the same!

MY PRAYER: Heavenly Father, thank You for giving me this

chapter on receive. I pray for the men who read this would understand what it means to receive from You, Lord. I thank You for Your gifts that You so freely give. You give us love, grace, mercy, forgiveness, and so much more. These things, I know we can never earn, therefore You freely give to us and all we need to do is receive them. I pray Lord, that where men struggle and are weak in receiving, that You would help them. Strengthen that area so they will not be lacking while walking this journey with You. Give them the ability to receive, not only the gifts You have in store, but the things that are needed for them to mature and become the men that You intended for them to be. Lord, as the song says, "It's hard to believe that all we must do is receive, it's a sweet mystery, that all we must do is receive".

Thank You, Lord.
In Jesus name, AMEN!

CHAPTER ⌀19

SACRIFICE ⌀S

"For whoever wants to save their life will lose it, but whoever loses their life for me will save it." (Luke 9:24)

Really, God? You want me to write on sacrifice? I mean what do I, or any of us for that matter, really know about sacrifice? The only one that can really speak or write on this topic is Jesus, Himself. He was the ultimate sacrifice for this world. None of us would be here right now if it weren't for His unselfish act of sacrifice to save all of us from our wretched selves. Scripture says:

"For as by one man's disobedience many were made sinners, so by the obedience of one shall many be made righteous." (Romans 5:19)

This verse is talking about Adam and Jesus, by the way. We see that the obedience of one made us righteous, and His obedient act was Him giving His life for ours. This chapter is by no means trying to compare ourselves to Jesus, because no one can or will measure up to that sacrifice. But let me try another.

Genesis 22:2 Then God said to Abraham, "Take your son, your only son, whom you love—Isaac—and go to the region of Moriah. Sacrifice him there as a burnt offering on a mountain I will show you."

Have any of you sacrificed any children lately? I hope not, otherwise you'd be reading this book from prison. What I want you to see however is the importance of sacrifice. I showed two different examples out of the Bible; one sacrifice is to save humanity from their sins. The other was as a test of faith. Both of these are very extreme examples.

I know that some of you probably have a sacrifice story or two that you could tell. Sacrifice can be very hard, but it's one of those things that you just do because it's the right thing to do. The more you step out in faith and sacrifice the easier it becomes because you are then more willing to do it. Unfortunately, there aren't enough of us men living sacrificial lives. For so many men life is all about "me", the selfish act of what they can acquire in life at any cost. All of our actions stem from something inside us and we act upon those feelings. That's the easiest way to respond to anything, letting our feelings do the responding so we don't have to put much thought into being responsible for those actions. If you haven't noticed by now, everything in this book requires some sort of action, regardless of our feelings.

Sacrifice, as you may already know, is not a feeling.

There's even a phrase you might have heard if something doesn't sit right with someone. They may let you know by saying, "I'm not feelin' it." God didn't create us to make decisions or go through life allowing our feelings to dictate our actions. No, he made us to be mature, wise people who make decisions and go through life doing things because they are the right things to do, regardless of how we feel. I bring up feelings with this topic because some of you may get the word sacrifice confused with feelings as if you feel like sacrificing or not. You may think that it's a choice to do so or not to do so. One of the definitions of sacrifice I found is pretty interesting. This is what it says: "destruction or surrender of something for the sake of something else". That's exactly what the opening scripture is all about.

"For whoever wants to save their life will lose it, but whoever loses their life for me will save it." (Luke 9:24)

Our job as Christ followers is to sacrifice the life we have created for ourselves, for the life that God intended us to have. Of course, if we are realistic, this isn't something that happens as soon as you commit to Him. It does take some time to get to that point, right? How do we get there? How do we get to the point that our faith is like that of Abraham's; able to go so far as to sacrificing our only son? I believe God allows us to show ourselves faithful with various tests of sacrifice in our daily lives.

Those of you with kids know very well what it means to sacrifice pretty much daily, right? As the definition implies, sacrifice is anything that we give up for someone else. You know, instead of you getting those new shoes you've had your eyes on, your kids become the recipient of something special. Often times we have to sacrifice our wants for someone else's. Some parents go as far to say that they pretty much have given up everything for their kids. I know for a fact that I could have done much better at sacrificing in my household. There are so many times that I should have sacrificed something and I didn't. This is why I mentioned earlier, it takes time to get to the point of complete sacrifice.

There have been times when I sit in my quiet time and just think about all the times I blew it because of my selfishness. I had an excuse though. I only wanted things because I didn't have them as a kid growing up. I didn't get the things other kids had. Later in life, I still didn't have what others had, so when I got the chance to have things, I got things for myself. Sometimes I bought things at the expense of others, including my kids. Some excuse, huh? I had absolutely no excuse! I can tell you though that I had to learn this thing called sacrifice and once I began to understand it, I was able to see so much more of what God wanted me to see.

I believe a lot of you know about sacrifice in some form or another. Unless you are loaded, don't you have to sacrifice purchasing wants for needs sometimes? Oh, wait a minute, that's what they made credit cards for, right? Okay, my mistake. 99% of you are disciplined users of your credit cards and you use them wisely, I am sure. For the 1% of you who are not, maybe you should try sacrificing for a while so that you can get your spending under control; just saying.

The point I'm trying to make here is that most of you already know quite a bit about sacrificing in small ways here and there. For some of you, these financial type sacrifices might not be small. If you look at them in the grand scheme of things they pretty much are though. What about sacrifices that hurt a little. No, literally. You know the ones that you do to take care of God's temple.

"Therefore, I urge you, brothers and sisters, in view of God's mercy, to offer your bodies as a living sacrifice, holy and pleasing to God—this is your true and proper worship." (Romans 12:1)

This verse says, "offer your bodies as a living sacrifice, holy and pleasing to God." Our bodies are not our own, they belong to God, the One who created us. Whatever you want to do with the body that you have been given is not your decision to make. That is if you say you are a Christ follower and that you love Jesus. Everything that we are is supposed to belong Him, and that's where sacrificing comes into play.

How many of you actually stop and turn away from something because you believe it wouldn't be honoring to God? Satan has created all kinds of vices to get us to indulge instead of sacrifice. We know that we are supposed to honor God by taking care of our bodies, but yet we eat things that make us fat, and we don't exercise so that makes us sick. If you look around our country alone you will see the unhealthy lifestyles so many of us have created for ourselves. You can see just how extensive the damage really is. God created us to fill the earth, subdue it, and have dominion over all living things that move about the earth. Everything that you stick into your mouths (because it's so good and irresistible) you're supposed to have control over. It is not supposed to rule over you.

In order to honor God, we must put aside what makes us feel good and sacrifice it. That goes for anything that is not honoring God. This could be how we dress; what we poke into our skin, or even what we carve into your bodies. None of these things honor God and it definitely is not offering our self as a living sacrifice. "Why?" What do you mean, why? Is it not clear? You know, it seems like we honor more of the rules man has put into place than God's.

Did you know that "tagging" a building is against the law? This means if you get caught spray painting any part of a building that is considered desecrating that building. You can be arrested for that. So, why do we not get arrested when we desecrate God's holy temple, which are our bodies, when we "tag" them with tattoos? Point being, instead of doing what you want to do for whatever reason, think about what you are actually doing. The question shouldn't be, "Is it okay to do this or that?" It should be, "Is what I want to do honoring to God?" We sacrifice for the greater good, because it's the right thing to do. Sacrifice is always about doing it because, deep down inside, we know it's the right thing to do. It may not always be the most popular, or comfortable thing, but it is God's way.

In recent years, I have come to know sacrifice all too well. I've had the privilege to be in business for myself and several other business endeavors through the years. I've always loved starting a business from scratch and working hard to grow it into something that was fulfilling. I never allowed money to be the motivating factor. That could perhaps be why I never made a whole lot of it. I just enjoyed the hard work and freedom of being self-employed. I invested so much money and time through the years and I always thought I would finally be successful with at least something.

I mentioned earlier in the book that I was actually at it again with a great idea right before I started writing this book. To be honest, the businesses that I have started earlier on hit walls because of various reasons; most likely due to the lack of financial know how. One of the last businesses I started was five years and it was on its way to being successful. The product was in several mainstream cycling magazines and it even aired on a popular TV show called American Thunder.

I created this design for my Harley that I had at the time and it was one of a kind accessory. I guess it just wasn't meant to be, however because in the midst of it all, I had to sacrifice this for what God wanted me to pursue. I thought I could do the business and serve God. I was planning to do great things with the money we would make. But getting rich at the time was not what He wanted for me.

I will be honest, packing up everything that had anything to do with the business and putting it all in the dumpster, was one of the hardest things I have ever had to do. It still hurts even as I write about it. It seemed for the first time in my life I took a concept that I had created for my use and turned it into a real manufacturing business with advertisements and customers. My wife and kids were so proud to see the years of hard work and perseverance paying off. Then I threw it all into the dumpster! What!? Was I smoking something? Did something hit me in the head? No, not at all. The impression I received from God through the Holy Spirit was that the design was the wrong pursuit. It was not what I was supposed to do. I needed to put all my time and energy into seeking my purpose for Him.

It has not been easy for me since I sacrificed this one thing. But I believe since I desired God's will and purpose for my life, I am a better man for it. I am actually at peace with doing that. I gave up a pretty big opportunity to become a better servant to God and to become a better husband to my wife and a better dad to my kids. Talk about sacrifice. I might be poorer in the wallet for it, but I am much richer in life overall. I can finally live a life of real purpose, because the moment I knew who I was and why I was here, God began leading the way and there wasn't anything else to compare to that.

I'm not saying for any of you to go out and shut down your businesses, but what I am saying is for you to reevaluate where you are right now with God. Has He been impressing upon you to change what you're doing currently? Should you sacrifice what you're chasing after to receive from Him what He has been trying to give you? Jesus Christ sacrificed Himself for all of us; He died so that you and I could be saved. What are you willing to sacrifice for Him? If you're looking for a certain outcome to a certain situation, sometimes a simple sacrifice is the answer.

I've heard it said that you have to, "give up, to go up". Unless you're able to sacrifice and to give up, you're not going to get very far in this life. God honors you when you sacrifice for Him, and I believe people admire a sacrificial person, whether they are Christ followers or not. That part of you that allows you to sacrifice is the part that is connected to Jesus, this is what people need to see.

Let me share another way to look at sacrifice. I mentioned a little bit ago that you have to "give up, to go up". This is a leadership quote from "The 21 Irrefutable Laws of Leadership" by John Maxwell. I don't know if you know who John Maxwell is, but I would encourage you to check out a gamut of his books on leadership. This particular quote is from law #18 "The Law of Sacrifice" where it states that you need to be willing to make sacrifices in order to become a true leader. I want to close out this chapter with this: If you are to lead well, then there are four things that you need to know about The Law of Sacrifice:

There Is No Success Without Sacrifice – Every person who has achieved any success in life has made sacrifices to do so. Effective leaders sacrifice much that is good in order to dedicate themselves to what is best.

Leaders Are Often Asked to Give Up More Than Others – The heart of leadership is putting others ahead of yourself. It's doing what is best for the team. For that reason, leaders have to give up their rights. The cost of leadership: Leaders must be willing to give up more than the people they lead. Leadership means sacrifice.

You Must Keep Giving Up to Stay Up – Leadership success requires continual change, constant improvement, and on-going sacrifice.

The Higher the Level of Leadership, the Greater the Sacrifice – The higher you go, the more it's going to cost you. And it doesn't matter what kind of leadership career you pick. You will have to make sacrifices. You will have to give up, to go up.

It doesn't matter what you are trying to do or where you are going in life; in order to get there you have to sacrifice. There's no way around it. As a Christ follower we have the greatest examples of sacrifice in the Bible. These examples show the greatness of God and how He works in us and through us for His glory.

MY PRAYER:

Heavenly Father, thank You again for yet another chapter in this book. Lord, when I think of sacrifice I can't help but to think about Cain and Abel and how You received the sacrifice that Able gave to You because he made an effort to give You his best. Cain on the other hand, held back and gave You less than his best. That makes me wonder how many of us are like that today. How many of us only give You the leftovers instead of putting an effort in giving You the best; our all? I pray, Lord, that as men read this chapter and as they become more curious and begin to seek the answers in Your Word, I pray that they will begin to understand what biblical sacrifice is all about. Not just the sacrifice that we give to You, Lord, but the daily sacrifices our family, friends, and others expect of us. Give us a serving heart. I thank You for giving us an understanding on what it means to become more and more sacrificial. We want to sacrifice so that it is pleasing to You. Give us a heart of sacrifice! May we continue to seek You, Lord, for the answers and may we be open and receptive to what You prompt us to do.

Thank You, Lord!
In Jesus' name, AMEN!

CHAPTER 20
TRUST

"Trust in the Lord with all your heart and lean not on your own understanding." (Proverbs 3:5)

I'm not sure how many of you are getting what I'm laying down here thus far, but if you are getting it, then you will agree that everything discussed has been about God providing ways to become better men. If we follow what is written in the Bible and do what it says instead of just getting around to it, then we can reap the benefits of "doing" instead of "feeling".

We need to learn how to do what is right because it is the right thing to do regardless of how we may feel. It's like what we talked about in chapter 6 on forgiveness; we forgive first because God tells us to, but we also forgive because it's for our benefit, not the other person's. How many people miss that by staying mad at someone and not forgiving them? God put that in motion for our own good. What about all the other things we should be doing for our own benefit? Like maybe this current topic on trust? God established this for our benefit, if we would just get it.

I have learned that you can't put your trust in yourself or in another person according to Scripture.

"It is better to take refuge in the Lord than to trust in humans."
(Psalms 118:8)

The reason why is very simple. If we do it God's way, and trust that God knows best, we won't be let down, hurt or offended. If you are let down, hurt, or offended it is because you don't trust Him. The reason for this is because we have the ability to let ourselves down. People will let us down as well. It's a fact that can't be changed. What can be changed is not trusting in other people or in yourself, but in God.

God has made it so simple for us, but we do what we do because that's what we "feel" like doing. But as you know, when it falls through, the blame game begins. Let's say for instance, you're walking in the store and there's a sign in the aisle that says, "CAUTION – wet floor". You walk on it anyway because you just have to get that one thing on the shelf. Unfortunately, you slip and fall. At that moment, you want to blame the store for your slip, but you knew what the sign said, so why are you mad?

We do the exact same thing with God. All throughout Scripture He tells us how we should live, but we only half listen and then feel the consequences. Then we have the nerve to get mad at God. I'm sorry, but that's just not right. It's no different with trust. We are to trust Him and not lean on our own understanding, simply because that's what His Word says. Every day we put our trust in something that doesn't satisfy our desires. We may be under this false illusion that it does or it will, but if we are really honest with ourselves, we know that it doesn't.

What I am talking about are the things we reach for instead of reaching out to God. All of the things like smoking, over eating, drinking, drugs, spending, and even sex are things we put our trust in to give us momentary satisfaction. Therein lies Satan's trap. You trust in a drink to relax you, until it overtakes you and you get hooked. You're feeling down and stressed so you go shopping to lift your spirits. You tell yourself you deserve it. You trust that going shopping will give you that momentary release of stress, and maybe it does until every single time you get stressed, you repeat the cycle of shopping. Now you find yourself in debt up to your eyeballs. I could keep going on and on with different scenarios.

You might not realize that you put so much trust into things for momentary satisfaction, but you do. I do too. I'm positive that each of us has that one, two, or few things that we trust more than we should. Think about those things for a moment and tell me that they have not let you down. These things may have even taken you somewhere you had no idea you would be. Correct me if I'm wrong; maybe you planned all along to get hooked on sex; I know I surely didn't. Maybe you planned on drinking too much and driving, just to get pulled over and thrown in jail? Whatever your thing or things are, did you plan on them taking you so far down that road?

I believe a lot of the time we equate trust with comfort or "feeling" comfortable. If you "feel" comfortable, then you believe you "trust" that person or thing. I hope you don't believe that. Ask anyone who has been burned by someone. Every story I've ever heard, whether it is relational or of a business nature, they all say they felt comfortable with that person and so they thought they could trust them.

How many topics so far have we discussed that has someone, maybe even you, feeling something? Have we not yet learned that our feelings are in no condition to make a solid or mature decision? People always getting hurt because they trusted in someone or something. That will continue to happen until you learn to put your trust in God.

Every now and then I catch myself watching this show on T.V. called, "American Greed" and it's narrated by Stacy Keach. Have you guys seen this show? Well here's the short of it: American Greed covers stories about more common crimes such as medical fraud, money laundering, Ponzi schemes, embezzlement, insurance fraud, and murder. Host Stacy Keach narrates how each case started from beginning to end, with dramatizations, interviews with real life victims, and evidence recovered by respective agencies in charge of bringing each perpetrator to justice.

American Greed; some people will do anything for money. I bring this show up in particular because every single time I have watched it, I am blown away at just how overly trusting people are. I can't believe how people will just trust because an individual says the right things, looks a certain way, or lives in a certain area of town. If a man or a woman "seem" to be trustworthy, that's not enough.

People trust others so much nowadays that they are willing to give someone else their whole life savings! Here's what really gets me. After some of these people have been swindled, they hate and refuse to forgive because it's all the other person's fault. All because they put 100% trust in another person. If only we would not put so much expectation and trust in others, we would recover so much faster. We would be able to function in life without all this junk that we allow to get built up inside of us to the point where we need something to take away the pain. We allowed it to happen in the first place!

Do you see how it's like a crazy merry-go-round? If only we would do what we should, we wouldn't have to worry about any of these after effects. Honestly, in turn we wouldn't need anything else to make us "feel" better. Some of these people I mentioned from the show are so done with life that they don't even know how to move forward anymore. All they feel is devastation. I get that, but even more so, at that low point, shouldn't someone direct them to God? They need true healing.

On the show and in real life, I understand what the motivation is in certain situations. Some would say it was for comfort in the later years, but it boils down to, yes it's in the title of the show, "greed". The reactions of some of these people are so life altering that all they have left in them is revenge. Why does our American currency say IN GOD WE TRUST when the very thing people put their trust in is money? So many people would rather put their trust in the paper itself instead of the Creator of the paper. God has given us such a simple path to walk so we can avoid weeding through all the junk just to figure out who or what to trust. We need only to put our trust in Him.

I've heard people say that doing things God's way is much harder, as if doing it their way is any easier? Ha! I don't think so. If I ever come to a place in life where I believe that doing things my way is easier or better than God's, I might as well go ahead and jump, you know, like off the bridge! Ok, for real. God's way can be difficult at times, but I've learned that it's not only the right way, but it definitely is the better way. What makes it more difficult is usually because God's way goes against the grain of what we have been taught or shown through society.

In case you forgot or didn't know, **God's way was the original way and the way that we should have been going all along.** I know many of you, have a very hard time with trust. Our past situations and issues can affect us throughout our entire life if we let it. I had a very hard time with trust myself. If I can be completely honest with you, one of my worst trust issues was with blacks. You see, I am mixed.

My biological mother is white and my dad is black. As a child in Parkersburg, West Virginia, I did have friends of different races, including a black kid named Tyrone Taylor. I had others in my class and it was all good, but I didn't realize that I had any issues until much later.

I don't know why my issues with blacks didn't come about earlier, but I know it had to do with people that hurt me the most. Unfortunately, my dad, physically and verbally abused me. Then there was an uncle of mine and his friends who had me do sexual stuff. I can't forget about the baby sitter who did the same. The one thing they all had in common was... you guessed it. They were all black.

I believe my issues arose after I left home at 17 and hung around some of my German friends who had some military friends. Some of those military guys were black and they would hang out with the German women. It was known back then that blacks didn't treat the women very well. After not trusting blacks and basically being afraid of them, I finally started standing up to these guys and kicking their butts. I would eventually go into the Army and still not trust them. I would associate when necessary, but that was it. It would take a few years, but I would eventually get proper understanding. Just because a few black people hurt me doesn't mean the whole race would.

Something changed within me and I found myself dropping my defenses. I began trusting them just like I did everyone else. It took me about twenty years or so to get to that point. I have learned that I don't have to necessarily pick and choose who or who not to trust. I love everyone the same now and I just leave the rest up to God. What I'm saying is this: bad stuff happens all the time, and sometimes it will happen to you. That's where we are supposed to trust God. He has all the answers and solutions for us. We eliminate any fearful living or distrust by putting our trust in the One who is ALL knowing.

The problem perhaps isn't this or that person; it could because you are putting too much faith and trust in people and things. I added faith in there because trust is a by-product of faith. You can't say that you have faith and not trust too. If you're not trusting God, then I would suggest you take a look at your faith in Him. I also believe the more you begin to trust in Him, the more your faith in Him will grow. You see, trust and faith work hand-in-hand. It takes faith to trust, and when we trust it shows faith.

I'm thinking about everything that I have written so far.

I don't want you to think I'm saying to never trust again. If you're not thinking that, then good, but for those of you who might be, let me clear that up and say, that's not what I am saying. I do believe there are trustworthy individuals still out there, and as much as I want people to think of me as trustworthy, I know it is only true to a certain extent. The truth of the matter is if you believe that God is in control and you're not, then circumstances beyond our control happen. If that's true, then putting all your trust in an individual is definitely not the thing to do. There are just too many dynamics at play and/or a whole lot of what ifs.

When you put a lot of trust in someone or something and the situation doesn't play out the way you had planned, what happens? Exactly, you get mad at the individual. You tell them how they let you down, and how you trusted them, right? Right. All kinds of bad things happen when someone you trusted lets you down. That's only because you didn't first put your trust in God. Trusting God first allows that individual to be off the hook. Instead of hating them, or cutting ties, or breaking up, or burning bridges, or divorcing, or whatever your action may be, you forgive!

When you act in this manner your relationships stay whole. Now I'm not saying that the individual doesn't have to learn whatever it is he or she needs to learn, but at least you'll be able to correct that person with love, not with bitterness and anger.

"It is better to take refuge in the LORD than to trust in people." (Psalms 118:8 NLT)

Another issue with trust is this: too many of us don't trust that God created us for His purpose, just the way that we are, no modifications needed. Now we all have some issues that we need God to work out of us, but as far as the core of who we are, we are His creation and we're fine. The question then should be, why won't we, or why don't we trust that God made no mistake when he created us? God has a purpose and a plan for each and every one of us.

Another question could be this: why do we trust what society says we should be? Why do we let the world dictate what we as men should look like, or dress like, or where you should live, or what the perfect body is, or what car you should drive, or what food to eat? I'm getting tired with all that. Why? Doesn't anyone see how much it's costing? And I don't mean just financially. God wants to form you into the man that He created you to be. I mean you didn't create yourself, did you? Jesus paid the price for our lives so they don't belong to us. Our lives belong to the Creator, and if you would just *trust* Him, He will do a much better job than your own efforts. I know this is not going to happen overnight. I mean it took me almost 20 years to trust blacks because of some junk from my childhood. I do have a couple of excuse though.

My first excuse is I didn't have this book or anyone to talk to about my problems. Second, I wasn't a Christ follower yet. But, it did come to a point where I had someone to talk to and I did become a Christ follower. I had no room for excuses at that moment. What about you? What is your current excuse? Oh, I've got one! The church hurt me so I left. I can speak on that too, as I felt hurt and kicked to the curb by a couple of pastors in my church. I didn't leave though. I wasn't supposed to.

What I learned from it though was this: I wasn't supposed to put my trust in the church or in anyone leading the church. Look, pastors and leaders are people too, they make mistakes. If your trust is in God, and you know that God has you where you are supposed to be, then good. That's what you trust. Keep going and serving even more. God will take care of what needs to be taken care of.

It wasn't until later on that I believed God impressed upon me to go and speak with those pastors in love and I even apologized for any part that I may have played in the situation. Do you know what happened? They saw their error and thanked me for continuing to persevere and coming forward. I told them that it wasn't necessary to apologize because I forgave them long ago perhaps God allowed for the situation to happen exactly as it had. That's where trusting in God comes into play. He knows what we don't know, so why would I put all my trust in man? All I had to do was take my hurt to God and trust that He would work it all out.

I am so thankful that I didn't have to hold on to any resentment or bitterness. I didn't have to leave the church or burn bridges, all because I put my trust in God. He worked it all out. Oh yeah, I didn't mention. At first, it was not easy, and yes I was upset and angry, but I have a great wife that helps me. Sometimes when I go off the deep end and try to act in a way that's not Christ-like, she keeps me focused and grounded. Thanks Honey!

So, of course I had to lay my situation before God so He could work out my feelings and have me do the right thing. I obeyed, and the rest is history. I have a pretty good standing with these pastors today.

"Don't let your hearts be troubled. Trust in God, and trust also in me." (John 14:1 NLT)

Trusting God with this, but not with that won't work either, guys. You just can't say that you have faith and that you are fully surrendered to Him when you only trust Him with this, but not that. "I trust You with this Lord, but I'll take care of that on my own."

That is definitely the wrong answer. Oh, my bad. Maybe you are trying something new; something no one in the history of man has ever tried before. Ha! I'm ROTFL! I'm sorry for my crude sarcasm. But come on, giving and trusting God-only partial has never worked and it will never work. I used to ask my now adult kids when they were younger, "Do you think you are the first one to do what you are doing?" Like they invented something new in disobedience or something. God's Word has stood for thousands of years and it hasn't changed, but we have. There is nothing else on this earth that has stood the test of time like God's Word, but yet we tend to trust so many of those things that have changed. The very morals that this country was built on, where are they now? Constant change for our comfort no matter the cost. We have political leaders afraid to take a stand because it will cost them votes, and we somehow put our trust in these very people.

"Surely God is my salvation; I will trust and not be afraid. The Lord, the Lord himself, is my strength and my defense; he has become my salvation." (Isaiah 12:2)

When we can trust like this scripture implies, then we can truly live a life of no fears and no worries. In order to do so, we must get these words deep in us. We must step out in faith and just trust God.

"Fear of man will prove to be a snare, but whoever trusts in the Lord is kept safe." (Proverbs 29:25)

MY PRAYER:

Heavenly Father, Your word clearly instructs us to trust you, and to put our trust in you; Lord we as men need your help with this. After writing this chapter on trust, I pray that the men who have read it have a more clear understanding and willingness to trust all things to you. I believe not trusting you Lord, is us trying to be in control. Help the men to give up that control so that what you want for each of them can be carried out in a more intentional way. Forgive us Lord for trying to be in control of something we're not anyway; I believe in all things you are still in control, and you have a plan and a purpose for each and every one of your men. We have got to just trust you, God. You, who created the heavens and the earth, and all that lives on the earth. You, Lord love all that you have created, so of course you already know what our lives are supposed to look like if only we would get out of the way of ourselves and just trust you. When we don't trust you Lord, we let our flesh dictate our lives instead of allowing the holy spirit to guide and lead us. Please, God help men to get rid of what's hindering them to simply trust you more and more each day.

In Jesus' name, AMEN!

CHAPTER 21

USABLE U

"Now in a great house there are not only vessels of gold and silver but also of wood and clay, some for honorable use, some for dishonorable." (2 Timothy 20:20 ESV)

"Therefore, if anyone cleanses himself from what is dishonorable; he will be a vessel for honorable use, set apart as holy, useful to the master of the house, ready for every good work."
(2 Timothy 20:21 ESV)

As I write each chapter, I research each title. As I'm doing so God shows up when I write. What I mean is that as I have been writing, I've been getting impressions from Him on what to say. In order to accomplish this book, I have to allow myself to be "usable" by Him to get across what it is He wants me to share.

In chapter 16 we discussed purpose. In chapter 9 we talked about how we need to be intentional in seeking God's purpose for our life. But now we have to figure out how to put everything together and allow ourselves to be usable. Just knowing that you have a purpose and that you need to be intentional in finding out what that purpose is, doesn't mean you have reached success. We need to get into a place in life where we are actually being used by God. I'm praying as I am typing this. It's very important that I put into words what I believe God wants each of you to know about reaching that place where God can use *you*.

Let's take a closer look at the scripture above from 2 Timothy 20:21. It tells us that if you cleanse yourself from what is dishonorable, you can be a vessel for honorable use. I can tell you that I have struggled with this off and on for some time. I mentioned earlier how Man On Purpose came about and that for a long time I was very excited about the direction God was having me go. But, after some time I started to become discouraged. It seemed like nothing was happening. The ministry wasn't growing and I just wasn't getting the support I thought I needed.

The first thing I did was look in the mirror. I wanted to see if there was something that I needed to do. I would ask questions like, "God, am I praying enough? Am I serving enough? Am I supposed to be doing this ministry at all? God, am I the wrong guy for this?"

The questions just kept pouring out of me. The guilt and shame followed. I just wasn't right in my head with all that was happening at the time, so I shut it down. I cancelled my account and all the interviews for my blog-talk radio show. I got off all social medias as well. I took a job in my field and thought that if I would just work and make money, everything would be just fine. The reason why I struggled with this scripture is because of my sins. I figured, if I can't defeat temptation, who am I to talk to other men about overcoming their sins?

A few years ago, I so desperately needed someone to be accountable to, but no one would step up and be there for me. Not one guy! I was so upset and even angry about this. I was there for so many guys, but when I needed someone to share my struggles with no one came my way. I'm not blaming anyone, I'm just sharing what happened and how I felt during that time.

I kept asking God for someone, but no one came. The guys that were the closest to me, I guess they weren't as close as I thought they were. I remember reaching out to a pastor friend of mine. He set it up so that we could meet once a week for lunch. We met as planned for a few months and everything was cool until this one particular day. I recall going through a "woe is me" time and I was struggling with sexual temptations. I shared with my pastor friend what was going on and something in particular that was happening. Somehow he changed the subject and left me hanging. He began canceling the upcoming lunches one week at a time until he stopped calling all together. He stopped returning messages and texts too. I was floored! I had no idea what I did or said. I still can't put my thumb on the reason why it all ended.

You want to know the details, huh? You want to know what on earth I told him, don't you? Ok, since I'm supposed to be transparent, I'm going to tell you. Before I do, I want you to understand the reason I am sharing all of this under the topic of usable. First, I am sharing because it all played a huge part in where I am today. Writing this book and allowing myself to be usable is for His glory.

My biggest and most devastating issue I have struggled with has been sexual temptations. Although I haven't had any physical affairs in my marriage with Carrie, I however have not been faithful. I have watched porn and had masturbation issues. Now, during this onslaught of attacks from Satan, I would get attacked during my praise and worship time and sometimes during prayer time. I would get an erection and not even know why. Literally, you think it's funny. There I would be, worshiping and praying to God with an erection! What the heck is that all about? Who should I have talked to about that? Oh I know. How about a pastor? Well, in my case, that didn't turn out too good. I got kicked to the curb yet again.

Apparently something was wrong with me. I mean, you can't drink coffee out of a broken cup right? What good was I to continue on? This is what I thought. I felt that God could not use me in that current state. But here's the thing - Was that my state of mind or was it the truth?

As we go along in our journey of life, we come across all kinds of obstacles, right? So, if we make some mistakes along the way, does that mean that we are no longer usable? Does God still have a calling on our life? These are some of the questions I wanted to ask someone of higher authority or someone with more wisdom. Maybe if I had an accountability partner, I would have ran it past him.

This is what I believe. I believe that only God can determine when He is ready to use you. How He does that is up to Him, but He has to be the One leading the way. When we go through everything that we go through and persevere, we eventually get to the point where we are fully usable.

I remember earlier in my walk with God, how I so desperately wanted to be used by Him to do something great and give Him the glory. In prayer, I would tell God to please use me however He chooses. I prayed this for years. But at that time, I didn't even know what my purpose was. I was lacking so much. I thought the areas that I was weak, He would be strong. That is true, and He was, but I was a bit more than weak. I was under-trained. My wife would assure me that there is definitely a "method to the madness". It seemed more like madness at the time, but God knew exactly what He was doing.

The thing is, you don't become a Christ follower today, and the next day start a men's ministry. Empowering men to become the men they are intended to be with purpose, on purpose takes time. Anyhow, I had no clue that's what my purpose would be. Truth be told, I thought Carrie and I would have a homeless ministry with a homeless shelter in Gwinnett County, Georgia. What I've learned from that experience was that particular ministry was only one piece of many other pieces in my "usable" puzzle.

Do you know that God uses everything to get you to that place where you can be usable? It's true. He uses not only your successes, but also your failures. He even uses what others were supposed to do in your life, but didn't. Nothing goes to waste or is irrelevant. The bad stuff goes right along with the good, as does the good stuff right along with the bad. What I'm learning on this journey is that our resistance comes from Satan trying to keep us from being used by God. Why do you think so many church pastors fall, or anyone else that is doing God's kingdom work?

Do you think before God gave me my purpose I was attacked as much? I can tell you no. I'm sure many of you know exactly what I'm talking about. To be usable for God's work is great, but it is not always easy, as I mentioned. It takes much prayer, meditating in the Word, obedience, and perseverance, to name a few.

Putting your faith and trust in God has to be what you live for. I've shared with you a few things that I struggled with in the past trying to being usable. What about now? I mean I'm still here, still seeking God in the areas I'm supposed to pursue and what I am supposed to be doing. I did have another go at the blog-talk radio show, but it just wasn't the same. Something just wasn't right. So, yet again I got off the air, which over time led me to continually seek Him on what to do with Man On Purpose. And that's how writing this book came about.

I have to believe this is exactly what God wants me to, at this moment be usable for. If you happen to read my testimony at the back of the book, you'll come to know more about my background and the directions I have walked in. I ultimately created who I became because of my past. I always enjoyed the scholarly things as a child, but I never became well developed in that area as much as I could have. It's funny how so many years later, God would have me doing some of those scholarly things I enjoyed as a child, but now for Him.

I never had the thought cross my mind to start a ministry; I wanted to start a business. I never planned 100% of the things that I have been doing since becoming a Christ follower. I never planned to have a radio show, or be on television talking about Man On Purpose, and I never planned on writing this 26-chapter book! I may not have succeeded, according to society's terms, in anything, but what I know today is that being successful in the world's eye is not the same as being usable in God's kingdom. I believe being usable by God carries much more weight than what my position in the world is. Now, don't get me wrong, again I say that God can use anyone anywhere. If you are in a highly successful position, then that's where you are and God can still do whatever He wants with you. The key is, you must be willing to have Him use you. Therein lies a problem though, or should I say could lie a problem. A lot of times guys in those highly successful positions aren't willing to let God use them because they might not have that highly successful position anymore, if you get what I'm saying.

How many of you in those positions are willing to risk your positions for what God may want you to do? Don't tell me all the bla, bla, bla about you having to make a living. There are other ways to do that. You have to be willing to be usable. Are you even in the right state of mind where God wants you to be so you can walk in your purpose and be usable? I've heard so many guys say they want to be used by God, but when it came right down to it, they weren't even willing to sacrifice. You know like all these A, B, C's that we have been discussing?

This is what I know to be true: if you are in a position with your job or career and it is far from God's best, and you know that you are not being used for His kingdom, guess what? You will go through the rest of your life missing out on God's best for you. Notice I said "best".

Remember when I mentioned Cain and Abel? Abel gave His very best and Cain only gave what he felt like giving. Whose offering did God accept? You can't say that you want to be usable by God and only give Him what you feel like giving to Him. I'm not saying that God hasn't used you in other areas here and there, because God can use everything, and I believe He does. If you are only giving God part of you, how's that working out? If you are honest and truthful with yourself, you would answer by saying it's not going as well as it could, or as it should.

What has God told you that you know you should be doing for Him? Stop making every excuse in the book and just go ahead and make it happen! I brought up the whole career/job thing because this is one of the main things a lot of men hide behind. The excuse is always that they have to make a living and provide. I get that. You think I don't know that all too well myself? When I first lost my position with Marriott I was devastated, to say the least. Then for months, God didn't open any other doors for another job. I spent money that we didn't have for the John Maxwell leadership training and then started Man On Purpose and a men's event...

Oh and let me add to that. While all this was happening, I was receiving unemployment. While I was paying for the leadership training, my wife had to work a second job! Yes, that's right. Talking about feeling like less than a man! I fought it as long as I could, but Carrie said that it was what God wanted, and I had to concur. I had to submit to what God wanted us to do. I know in the "man world" this is a definite, big, fat "NO". God's ways are not our ways, that's what we have to remember.

How many opportunities have you let pass by simply because your "man pride" got in the way? Stop trying to figure everything out and just let God work. The smartest and most intelligent person on this earth still is thousands and thousands of miles away from ever trying to figure out God. Being usable by God does not look anything like you have ever seen, or anything you have ever done, or anything anyone else has ever seen or done.

A good friend of mine Stephen Verner and his wife Brandy have stepped up to the challenge and have allowed themselves to be usable for God in a way that they never dreamed. You see, they have been called to Italy with a ministry they have founded called "Wake Up, Italy". They have been in this 8 year process getting prepared for that day when they will finally see a huge part of their vision come to pass. Both Stephen and

Brandy were professional staff members at Victory World Church, working and serving in the church, and asking God to use them in a way that would glorify Him. How were they supposed to know that serving in the apartment ministry would lead them to Italy on a vision trip and then ultimately starting up a ministry of their own where they would end up *living in* Italy and ministering to the lost people there? They are slated to pick up and move in August, 2015. I can tell you that it has been a blessing to me to watch their story unfold. I'm sure some of you have amazing testimonies as well.

These are the things that happen when you and I open ourselves up to God and let Him use us in the way that He has planned. Things aren't always going to follow a specific pattern, the way everyone else thinks that it should. Look at what it says here in Scripture:

"For my thoughts are not your thoughts, neither are your ways my ways," declares the Lord. As the heavens are higher than the earth, so are my ways higher than your ways and my thoughts than your thoughts." (Isaiah 55:8, 9)

What it's saying here is that who are you and I to question something that God is doing in someone's life? Can you know the thoughts of our Creator? Can you know His plans for someone else or how He wants to carry them out? If I'm honest with you guys, I remember Stephen talking to me about them moving to Wheaton, Illinois to get their graduate degrees and I was thinking for what? I mean they were still fundraising and they already had people who were supporting the ministry financially, my wife and I included. It didn't make any sense to me. Why would any of us want to support you guys while you go to school? They believed in their hearts they were doing the things that God wanted them to do, and so they packed up what they could fit in their car that had over 240,000 miles on it and drove from Atlanta to Wheaton, Illinois with their 2 kids, Laynie and Bryson.

Once they graduated and came back to Georgia, God opened new doors for them and positioned them exactly where they needed to be in order to accomplish all that they were called to accomplish. They continue to stay true and faithful to the vision that God gave them and soon they will find themselves at the next leg of this amazing race.

Where do you find yourself right now in your journey? Are you more concerned about your mortgage or career? Are you still telling yourself that you'll do "it" when the time is right? What has God been telling you to do that you have not obeyed? Have you even started preparing yourself to be used by God? If you haven't, what are you waiting for?

MY PRAYER:

Heavenly Father, thank You so much for being with us on this journey. I know that we can't do this without You. You have stirred our spirit to the point where we want to be used by You and for You only. We want to honor and glorify Your Holy name. I don't have all the answers as to how we're going to accomplish what we're supposed to, but I believe that as long as we stay faithful and seek You, all of our answers will come. I pray, wherever we are lacking wisdom that You will provide us with Your wisdom to know and discern Your promptings. Lord, we give ourselves over to You and ask that You will continue working in us. Change us into the men that You intended us to be with purpose, on purpose. I thank You, God for everything that You are and for all that You are doing. Each day that we are given, I pray that we put ourselves in a position to be used by You. I thank You on behalf of the men for allowing us to be usable.

In Jesus' name I pray, AMEN!

CHAPTER (22 V)

VISION

"Where there is no vision, the people perish." (Proverbs 29:18 KJV)

I know exactly what you're thinking. You're saying to yourself right this second, "Oh brother, not again. I've heard this scripture preached on and talked about more than a thousand times." I know some of you thought that, because I thought the same thing too. I tried to tell God that maybe we should look for another "V" word, just sayin'. I mean, the moment a message about vision pops up, so does this verse; like every single time. But let's just see where He wants to take us with this.

I've already told you guys that I have to follow His lead. What He says goes. Obviously this is still considered a very important topic so let's roll with it. I will stick my neck out there and say that having vision is so very important, not just because it truly is, but also because so many of us are not getting it. I said *us* not you. I fail at this sometimes too.

What I mean by failing is understanding and knowing what God's vision for me is versus what I believe it to be. I guess some of you might be wondering if a vision is the same as a dream. I believe that vision is the part that gets put into action from a dream. A vision however does not have to come from a dream. You could have several dreams that don't really mean much in the grand scheme of things. Or perhaps God could give you a dream that calls for some sort of action. This is where vision comes into play when things get dark. This is where you have to turn on the headlights so you can see where you are going.

If you read the stories in the Bible about the individuals that had dreams, their dreams came to past because some kind of action took place. Look at Joseph and his dreams. His brothers mocked and made fun of him, and they began to dislike him so much so that they sold him off. Would you know it; his dreams finally came true some 13 years later. But they came true! Joseph only had to be obedient and follow the flow of what was happening in his life. As he became overseer, I believe God gave him vision so that he would become successful in whatever he did for God. Vision is what God gives you so that you know what you should be aiming toward. I believe this to be a personal encounter between you and God. No one else can dictate to you something God has given to you.

A vision is supposed to keep you on track with His purpose for your life. God has created all these intricate details of how things were supposed to be, but man decided to change things up to accommodate convenient living. Instead of seeking God for His vision for us, we have allowed all these other things to influence us. I call them distractions. If you look around, you can put a name to the ones that are blocking your vision.

The Bible is full of encounters with God through dreams and visions. To this day, it is still very much a common way that God communicates with those He chooses to communicate with. The vision that God wants or has for you can't always get to you because of things in your way. For instance, what you watch, read, or listen to plays a huge part in being capable of receiving vision from God. How are you going to run a marathon if you are still scarfing down junk food and sucking down sodas? You can't continue on that kind of a diet and expect to get any great results, or even finish the race. It's the same with receiving what we need from God. If you are not living the lifestyle that God has called you to live, how can you expect to hear, or see anything that God is trying to show you or say to you?

Now, I'm not saying that you have to arrive or anything like that. If that were the case, then none of us would ever get anything from God. We will never arrive at anything until Jesus comes back. I am saying that God does have a purpose for you and He has to convey that to you some kind of way. So, wouldn't it be wise to be looking out for it. He can give you a vision right this minute, but remember it doesn't mean that it's all going to come together right now.

That's a mistake I have made a few times. When I have a dream or a vision, I get started right away. But when it doesn't work, I get upset. All the while, God is saying, "I gave you a vision; something to work toward, something that is to happen in the future." Those of us that are able to see the picture of the puzzle before it is actually complete is a gift from God.

For some of you, you may be capable of having vision in your jobs on a daily basis. I know project managers, for example, have to be able to see the complete project from start to finish. Great leaders have great vision as well. I believe as we mature, our ability to see gets better. But here's the thing that has been getting me for so long. I mentioned it a little bit ago. Discerning what is what.

Do you know what I mean by that? You know, trying to figure out what exactly we're supposed to have vision for. For myself, most of my life I have wanted to have my own business and/or be self-employed. That was my personal vision for my life. I even left the Army early to pursue a business that I had a passion for. My very first "business" venture, happened when I was only 10 years old. I created a product and sold it. I didn't stick with it very long, but that's a business venture right?

One season of my life, I left a great paying territory manager job to start an auto detailing business. I had no savings, and no customers. All I had was this vision that I could make better money than what I was making at that time. I worked hard and stuck with my vision for success. I went from having no equipment to having everything I needed in a few short months. My customer base grew like crazy. I even came close to getting a permanent location, as that was part of the vision.

I've gotten this far with several different ideas. I would have an idea and I would just go for it. As I would begin my project, the vision would begin to get clearer and clearer. I would keep going in that direction until I would hit a wall and couldn't go any further. The vision was still intact, but knowing how to overcome the obstacles was another thing. I was not a Christ follower for most of those years, therefore I had nowhere to turn. I did everything on my own. Did you know that the projects that you envision don't happen all by yourself? It takes a team to make a vision successful. A team of people.

Truthfully though, even as a Christ follower, I still struggled with wanting to do "my thing". I had to come up with ways to make a living during the times I had lost my job. They somehow always came to an end. I couldn't figure out what the deal was with all these temporary start-ups? One of my biggest endeavors yet was five years in the making. I started it before I came to know Christ and continued with it as my relationship with God grew. I truly believed that it was God who gave me the idea and the vision to make this happen. The business I'm talking about is where I designed floorboards, passenger pegs, brake pads, and shifter pegs for my Harley. I made the decision that it would be a great business.

Carrie and I put everything in the making of "r2 Concepts" and we both were amazed at how far we had come since getting our vision in line with God's. Boy, were we wrong. I remember after the items were introduced on the TV show, American Thunder, how I cried. I was so excited and I felt accomplished. I just knew that God had blessed us! I had a strong belief that He was going to work miracles just so we could be a testimony on his behalf. My vision was huge for this company. I had 15 more designs that I wanted to manufacture. God had other plans though.

Shortly after our initial product got messed up by the chromer and powder coater, we didn't have any more money for new stock. I began to question if something wasn't right. How could God have been with us for so many years and allowed the products to be in magazines and on TV, but our units were not moving like we were told they would? Any company that goes on American Thunder doubles or triples their orders. This was supposed to be an instant success situation. "God, why? God, what is going on?" How many of you have been there? How many of you are there right now?

That's why I share this story with you. Many of you have talents and a desire to do something, yet nothing, and I mean nothing is happening. You hear from others to follow your heart's desires and let your passion drive you, but then what. You can have well drawn designs, or well thought out plans that includes a great vision, but if that's not what God's vision is for you, guess what?

What I am saying is only in the case that you have already surrendered your will over to God. If you are telling God that it's His way and not yours, then you are in it 100%. Only when God is first, then His will can be done in our life. It doesn't matter what makes sense, or what looks like it should work. How much money you could earn and put towards His kingdom to help others don't move God either. If God hasn't signed off on the vision, it just won't work.

That's what I figured out on one specific dreary day. I had been in prayer about what to do and I shared it with Carrie. She told me that I needed to do what I believed God was telling me to do. So I did. I packed up everything from my business, r2 Concepts, and put it all in the dumpster. I had to make a commitment to God that I would follow what He wanted for me, not what I wanted for me.

You see, this was so very hard to do. I'm just a little nobody from Parkersburg, West Virginia and I wanted to amount to something; you know, be *somebody*. That has been my vision all my life. Yet when the chance came about to possibly make it big, none of that mattered anymore. I am already somebody in God's eyes. You are somebody in God's eyes too. That's what matters. In order to see the vision, we have to find our identities in Him, not in anything else. The commitment we make to God has to line up with the vision, then you will be on your way to true fulfillment.

Instead of saying, "I can't" or "It's too hard", how about giving it over to God and let Him help you? When we mentally prepare ourselves to be used by God and for His use, we become intentional with seeking His purpose for our lives. This then enables us to envision our course of action and stay on that path. This then brings forth true fulfillment in life.

Instead of fighting against the current, go along with the current that God has already established. If you do this, I believe you will see a huge difference in your life.

My own vision for my life could have possibly led me to making lots of money and who knows what else, but I know for a fact that I would not be the same man that I am today had I continued in my own pursuits. I'm not saying that it's wrong to make money. I'm saying that if making money had consumed my life, making more of it would have left me with a hole inside that money can't fill. That's why I had to stop for a moment and ask, "Is this what I am supposed to be doing, Lord? Is this Your vision for my life?

Everything God has had me write in this book is like 26 teeth in a cog system. Each tooth interlocks with another cog to create forward momentum. If one of the teeth is damaged, or doesn't feel up to the task on a particular day, then the whole system isn't working as efficiently as it could. I mean, yeah, you can have a few messed up teeth and the cog can still turn and move forward, but not for long. Eventually the whole system will break apart. The same goes for what we need in order to fulfill what we are put here on this earth for. That is why vision is so important.

Vision is what allows you to see the bigger picture; or sometimes just smaller pieces of the bigger picture. Nonetheless, it's what should be driving you to get out of bed each morning. The vision of making something happen for God's kingdom in a way that only He can have you do. If you do not know where you are going, it's because you have no vision. I believe that right now is a great time to join me in the prayer at the end of the chapter. It is time to ask God to give you eyes to see His vision for your life.

MY PRAYER:

Heavenly Father, first of all, thank You, Lord for this chapter. I thank You for all the men that have and will be reading this chapter. I lift up every man who has gotten to this point and has come to the realization that they have swayed from the vision that you have for them. I pray with the men and ask You, Lord for forgiveness. Anywhere we have not been true in our walk with You that has hindered our vision. Just getting by, day by day, is not what You want for us. You have great things in store for us and we only need to seek Your purpose and get Your vision for our lives. Forgive us for trying to do it ourselves and not leaning on You. I pray that men would realize true identity and fulfillment come only when we are living surrendered lives to You. Lord, I know that I surely don't have the answers for these men, but I know that You do. I lift up these men to you, believing that they would open themselves up to Your Holy Spirit in prayer for the answers they need. May this prayer, be a starting point for the men around the globe to see the vision for their lives, with Your eyes.

In Jesus' name, AMEN!

CHAPTER 23
WISDOM · W

"Get wisdom, get understanding; do not forget my words or turn away from them. Do not forsake wisdom, and she will protect you; love her, and she will watch over you. The beginning of wisdom is this: Get wisdom. Though it cost all you have, get understanding." (Proverbs 4:6-7)

Just how important is wisdom? Isn't intelligence enough? I believe that wisdom is of the utmost importance and intelligence alone won't suffice. To get a better understanding of wisdom, I decided to look it up and see what the Merriam-Webster Dictionary had to say.

Wisdom -

: knowledge that is gained by having many experiences in life

: the natural ability to understand things that most other people cannot understand

: knowledge of what is proper or reasonable: good sense or judgment

If you noticed, there's nothing about intelligence in any of those definitions. Can you have wisdom, but no intelligence? I don't believe so. I found this article entitled, "All About Wisdom" in Psychology Today, check it out.

It can be difficult to define wisdom, but people generally recognize it when they encounter it. Psychologists pretty much agree it involves an integration of knowledge, experience, and deep understanding that incorporates tolerance for the uncertainties of life as well as its ups and downs.

There's an awareness of how things play out over time, and it confers a sense of balance. Wise people generally share optimism that life's problems can be solved and experience a certain amount of calm in facing difficult decisions. Intelligence — if only anyone could figure out exactly what it is – may be necessary for wisdom, but it definitely isn't sufficient; an ability to see the big picture, a sense of proportion, and considerable introspection also contribute to its development.

According to this, intelligence or even knowledge is not what defines wisdom. I mean, how many smart kids do you know that continually do stupid things? How many smart adults do you know that continually do stupid things? The reason for this, especially in our kids is they lack wisdom. The same goes for adults who keep doing the same dumb things over and over. Age isn't a precursor to wisdom either; not necessarily. I believe experiences in life are what attributes to wisdom.

Mistakes made, lessons learned, and wisdom gained.

Well, that's one way to gain wisdom. It's probably the most common way. Nothing wrong with gaining wisdom this way, it just takes a little longer doesn't it? Do you believe that age isn't a precursor to wisdom? Well, wisdom actually is supposed to come with age, but unfortunately we have too many grown up individuals who call themselves "mature men" with no more wisdom than some 20 year-olds. The older one gets, the wiser one becomes is no longer a blanket statement. I know for me, I had to ask God for wisdom. I believe with enough teaching and study one can become pretty "smart" or intelligent, but the wisdom we need to carry out God's assignments can only come from Him and in His time.

As I become more "mature" in Christianity, I know I need wisdom to be able to make right decisions; Christ-like decisions. I believe through all my circumstances I have attained some sort of wisdom, but that wasn't enough as time would tell. It's one thing to have someone tell you about something and another to have done it yourself. I believe you can learn from listening, but wisdom comes from the actual experience of doing it.

If you think about it, wisdom is kind of like faith. Faith is something you either have or you don't have. Faith can be cultivated and grown over time. The closer you are to God and experience evidence of His existence, the more your faith will grow. Wisdom is just like that. Through your experiences, whether failures or successes, over time you gain wisdom.

What you did not know with your first child, you know with your second child. Why? Because experiences with the first child taught you things that you can use with your second child. This is growth, nevertheless, it is also called wisdom in which you have attained from experience. Now, if you did the same things with your second child as you did with your first child, knowing they didn't work, then that's not wisdom. Wisdom tells you to take what didn't work and come up with an alternate way of handling the situation. Why does wisdom tell you this? Because you know from past experience what should work.

Wisdom also tells you to be open minded. You don't want to be rigid in thought because you may have to resort to an alternate solution. Wisdom is the ultimate when it comes to making decisions and finding solutions. I believe wisdom will always win over knowledge. Why do I believe that? Because knowledge alone is not sufficient.

Wisdom is so valuable that the Bible talks about it extensively. There's even a whole book written that is considered the "Book of Wisdom" which of course is Proverbs. One of my favorite examples in the Bible about the importance of wisdom comes from 1 Kings where God tells King Solomon that he can have anything he wants. Take a look at how he responds to God:

"At Gibeon the Lord appeared to Solomon during the night in a dream,

and God said, "Ask for whatever you want me to give you." Solomon answered, "You have shown great kindness to your servant, my father David, because he was faithful to you and righteous and upright in heart. You have continued this great kindness to him and have given him a son to sit on his throne this very day. Now, Lord my God, you have made your servant king in place of my father David. But I am only a little child and do not know how to carry out my duties. Your servant is here among the people you have chosen, a great people, too numerous to count or number. So give your servant a discerning heart to govern your people and to distinguish between right and wrong. For who is able to govern this great people of yours?" The Lord was pleased that Solomon had asked for this. So God said to him, "Since you have asked for this and not for long life or wealth for yourself, nor have asked for the death of your enemies but for discernment in administering justice, I will do what you have asked. I will give you a wise and discerning heart, so that there will never have been anyone like you, nor will there ever be. Moreover, I will give you what you have not asked for—both wealth and honor—so that in your lifetime you will have no equal among kings." (1 Kings 3:5-13)

Now, what if that had been you? When I read these verses from time to time, I often ask myself what would I have chosen. Think about it for a moment. Do you understand just how important and valuable wisdom really is? I bet that if you are one of today's twenty something's you are sharing more knowledge than wisdom. I know society teaches that knowledge is power, but wisdom, my friends, triumphs knowledge every time. Knowledge is about the "knowing" of something, whereas wisdom is the "knowing" of something plus the "experience" of something. This is why Solomon indirectly asked God for wisdom.

You see, according to various commentaries Solomon was most likely one of those twenty somethings. He knew that the only way to rule over God's people properly was with wisdom. Worldly wisdom would take too long to attain through experience. He needed wisdom now, at that moment, more than anything else. This is what we call godly wisdom. He knew that with God's help, all things were possible. He wanted to rule God's people the right way and the best way that he could.

Every day you and I have to make decisions on things that require wisdom. There are too many of us guys going along in life simply saying and doing whatever we want with no thought about the consequences. Wisdom teaches us to think things through. Wisdom is for those who are mature enough to receive it, not necessarily only for those who are old enough. Solomon was young in age, but mature enough in mind to be able to even ask for wisdom.

One night I was watching the show LOCKUP on TV and there was a young guy talking about how he had attained some wisdom from some of the guys there in the jail. I was like, "Really? Just about everyone in jail is there because of a lack of wisdom. You're telling me you've attained it?"

If these guys had any bit of wisdom, they wouldn't be repeat offenders. A very small percentage actually get out and allow for some sort of wisdom to help them change their ways. Wisdom tells us *not* to do something even though we might *like* doing it. Wisdom says not everything we like in life is something we need to do in life. That's wisdom for you.

As married men, wisdom should tell us not to engage in personal conversations with other women. That same wisdom should tell you married men not to present yourself as available. Wisdom should be telling you that spending absurd amounts of money on extracurricular activities is not a wise thing to do. Wisdom can tell you all kinds of things to keep you out of trouble; the key is this: listen when she speaks!

As I mentioned before, wisdom does not always line up with our wants and desires. It doesn't have to. It is in our best interest to do what's wise. Wisdom can be our best friend, if we just let "her", as the Bible calls wisdom, guide us through life. When you come to a place where you have to debate back and forth with yourself about something, instead of telling yourself that you deserve it, or that you've earned it, ask yourself if it's the wise thing to do.

Wisdom will always put others first. Regardless of the situation, when you are dealing with an individual that said or did something, before confronting that person, ask yourself what is the wise thing to do? I had a situation with Josh, our twenty-one-year-old. He is the youngest of Carrie's four kids that we raised together. I've known Josh since he was nine years old, now he is a very intelligent young man. He is one of those guys that was bored in school because he was more advanced than some of the others. Unfortunately, instead of doing what he needed to be doing, he would act up in class which would hinder any teacher from wanting to put him in advanced classes. He became known as the troublemaker in class. Josh at the time, although smart, was not too wise.

I have been watching him throughout the years and he has continued to show this same pattern. He's all grown up now; filled with intelligence, but lacking true wisdom. His behavior has really been getting to me because I know his potential and we've even had a few fall-outs because of it.

The other day I needed to call him and talk about a certain situation that he got himself into. I really didn't want to call him, but I did it anyway. Wisdom has taught me to not stop being a parent to him, specifically a dad. He wants me to call him out in a respectful, loving way. He will respond if my words influence him and encourage him to do what he needs to do. Wisdom has taught me that the end result is what's important.

Wisdom has also taught me that when I don't know how to approach a situation, the best thing to do is: PRAY. So that's what I did. The conversation with Josh went very well. He was receptive and he did exactly what he needed to do to get out of his situation. The conversation was nowhere as bad as he initially thought it was going to be.

Mistakes made, lessons learned, and wisdom gained.

When I left home at the age of 17, if God had offered me an opportunity to receive a gift from Him, wisdom would have been a great one to choose.

"When I was a child, I talked like a child, I thought like a child, I reasoned like a child. When I became a man, I put the ways of childhood behind me." (1 Corinthians 13:11)

Again, this is wisdom speaking. Children don't have much wisdom at all, so their behaviors are understandable. As you mature into manhood, wisdom should be sought after. This is what will help you put away childish things. Wisdom says, "Hello! It's time to put down the Xbox controller and go help your wife with something."

As a matter of fact, being a grown man, wisdom should be telling you to get rid of the Xbox all together. As a man, wisdom should be telling you to stop letting the woman do all the child raising and get involved in the family affairs. I think you get the point? I'll end this chapter with more scripture.

"Who is wise and understanding among you? Let them show it by their good life, by deeds done in the humility that comes from wisdom. But the wisdom that comes from heaven is first of all pure; then peace-

loving, considerate, submissive, full of mercy and good fruit, impartial and sincere." (James 3:13, 17)

Who is wise and understanding among you? Are you showing your wisdom by deeds done in humility that comes from it? One of the ways to help in this journey with Jesus is to get the wisdom that we have been discussing in this chapter. If you don't have it, then simply ask for it. Remember chapter 1: Ask? How will you receive if you don't ask?

MY PRAYER:

Heavenly Father, thank You, Lord for this amazing opportunity to share with men about wisdom. The kind of wisdom that can only come from You. I pray that a word, a line, or a verse that the men read will stir their heart to seek this kind of wisdom; the kind that can allow men to make better decisions in their journeys with You. Lord, may we all be like Solomon and ask You for wisdom over anything else. I pray for all the men today that they too will have the courage to pray this prayer over other men. May they receive the wisdom that they need to fulfill their purpose that You have for them. I believe, Lord in the name of Jesus that You will grant us this request. By faith, we thank You in advance, Father.

In Jesus' name, AMEN!

CHAPTER 24
XCELLENCE X

"Whatever you do, work at it with all your heart, as working for the Lord, not for human masters." (Colossians 3:23)

Excellence – the quality of being outstanding or extremely good.

In today's society, it seems that this word pertains to some things and not to others. Let me say it like this: it depends on what line of work you are in. Some jobs require nothing but excellence, and others, not so much. As the chapter verse says, we should be excellent in everything we do. Notice it does not say to "be perfect" in all we do. I guess some could argue that this verse says nothing about excellence. I believe that if you do something from the heart, that's about as excellent as one can be.

Are you excellent in all you do for God? Do you work to glorify yourself or to glorify God? Being excellent for God means to put Him first in all your decisions. If you were being excellent for God, you would acknowledge that He put you in your position, thus you would be striving to honor God because the opportunity came from Him. Does that make any sense to anyone? Let me try and clarify what I'm trying to say here. A lot of the time people find themselves in jobs or positions that they don't like. They only work there to pay the bills. Individuals who have this sort of attitude usually don't strive to be excellent. This is because, instead of seeking God for guidance, you take whatever job to pay the bills. Sadly, you end up not being happy and your work or performance suffers because of it.

What we need to be striving for is excellence on our job or in any situation, instead of just getting by. If you do find yourself somewhere you don't want to be, change your attitude about it. Opposed to being sour or angry, be content and understanding; not for yourself or even for the employer, but for God.

Whether you are in a situation that you like or hate, striving for excellence should not matter. We strive for excellence to be an example of who Jesus is. This should be a trait that is natural amongst Christ followers. If non-Christians can go after excellence with everything they have, what is the excuse for believers?

Excellence portrays who Jesus is. How can you or I claim to be followers of Christ, but yet do less than all the others? Possibly it's not your actions but maybe your attitude is what stinks. Another way to look at striving for excellence is found in a speech that Martin Luther King Jr.

gave. Here is an excerpt from that speech:

"And when you discover what you will be in your life, set out to do it as if God Almighty called you at this particular moment in history to do it. Don't just set out to do a good job. Set out to do such a good job that the living, the dead or the unborn couldn't do it any better. If it falls your lot to be a street sweeper, sweep streets like Michelangelo painted pictures, sweep streets like Beethoven composed music, sweep streets like Leontyne Price sings before the Metropolitan Opera. Sweep streets like Shakespeare wrote poetry. Sweep streets so well that all the hosts of heaven and earth will have to pause and say: Here lived a great street sweeper who swept his job well. If you can't be a pine at the top of the hill, be a shrub in the valley. But be the best little shrub on the side of the hill. Be a bush if you can't be a tree. If you can't be a highway, just be a trail. If you can't be a sun, be a star. For it isn't by size that you win or fail. Be the best of whatever you are."

- Martin Luther King Jr.

I just love this. Dr. King was talking about being excellent in whatever you do. You see, excellence is the quality of being outstanding or extremely good. It wouldn't be until later in life I would understand what my parents were trying to beat into me. I do literally mean "beat" into me. I had to do everything right, as my parents would say. They never really explained to me why I had to do everything right, they just wanted it done that way.

As I got older, you can imagine that the demands on my kids or others were pretty high. Everything I did I was trying to reach perfection, which I have long since learned is impossible. Striving for perfection is not the same as striving to be excellent. Being excellent in all that we do is attainable, while perfection is not. It took me many years to learn this though.

I remember how hard I worked to be the best I could be when I was in the U.S. Army. This was the first place I learned the difference between perfection and excellence. The work ethics which were instilled in me from my parents were already above and beyond, but I seriously needed to learn how to not kill myself striving to be perfect, or always trying to out-do everyone else. If someone was carrying one box, I would carry three boxes. If others worked for twelve hours straight that day, I would stay on for another six to eight hours. There were so many things that I did while in the military that showed I was really trying to be more excellent than others, and I was rewarded for those efforts by receiving all my rank with waiver.

What that means is this: I always received my next rank quicker than usual. For example, if I was supposed to be an E-2 for 18 months before advancing to E-3, my hard work and conduct allowed me to become an E-2 in less than 12 months. I received my next rank or pay grade to E-3 in a shorter amount of time. This happened as well when I got promoted to E-4. In all, I was promoted to E-5 in about 36 months. After E-4 you earn E-5 with points, which I achieved right before getting out, however I couldn't benefit from it because I had signed an early release. This was a bummer for me of course.

The point I'm trying to make is that I learned to put much value on being an excellent soldier rather than a perfect one. I accomplished so much in the short four years I served, all because I knew that I needed to be excellent. Although it didn't start out that way, I did have a little help grasping the concept. One day, a Staff Sargent, who believed in me, explained the importance of excellence. This is when I began to understand the difference between perfection and excellence.

Excellence is not just about how you perform your duties or work; it is about how you carry yourself in everyday life. As a Christian, excellence should be with you at all times. I had learned to be excellent at my job, but what about my character? Was I excellent in my character? Was I excellent in raising my kids? Was I excellent as a husband? I can tell you that I definitely was not! What about you? There are thousands of men who are excellent at whatever is important to them. How many of you are excellent at your jobs or careers, but are far from being an excellent husband? Are you even striving to be an excellent man, husband, father, or servant? Think about it.

If you're reading this book or any other books similar to this one, then I believe you are. That is what all 26 chapters are about. Putting everything to practice, to strive for excellence in everything, not just one thing or some things, but in everything we do. You being excellent in all things brings honor to your Creator.

"In the same way, let your light shine before others, that they may see your good deeds and glorify your Father in heaven."
(Matthew 5:16)

This verse just came to my mind. I read it and think about striving to be excellent so that others can see and know that it comes from God. The light of excellence should shine so bright in each and every one of us. Think about what you can do today to show others that you want to strive for excellence. Instead of wondering if that extra effort will count for something, just "do" and know that God sees it even if others don't.

I've learned that I don't need affirmation from men or women because God sees what I do, and He will reward me in a much greater way than any person ever could. When we act and choose to do the things that God has put in place for us to do, the rewards can be amazing. I promise you. I'm not necessarily talking about money or material things either. God rewards us however He chooses. It should be clear that God wants His people to abound or excel in both what they are (inward character) and in what they do (behavior or good deeds). Obviously, there is no way on earth than an individual can love God with all he is without striving to do his or her best. Since that is so, the pursuit of excellence is both a goal and a mark of spiritual maturity.

However, for this to be true, the pursuit of excellence must be motivated by the right values, priorities, and motives. If we go astray here, the pursuit of excellence can quickly become a mark of immaturity and just another result of man's obsession with his own significance, which, as mentioned previously, is a perilous pursuit.

Wrong motives equates to loss, whereas right motives equates to gain.

So then, biblically speaking, the pursuit of excellence refers to pursuing and doing the best we can with the gifts and abilities God has given us. It is our duty to give our best so that God and only God get the glory.

Ideally, attaining excellence should be done without the spirit of competition or seeking to be better than others. Excellence includes doing every day, common things, but in a very uncommon way, regardless if people are watching.

"Therefore, my dear brothers and sisters, stand firm. Let nothing move you. Always give yourselves fully to the work of the Lord, because you know that your labor in the Lord is not in vain."
(1 Corinthians 15:58)

PURSUING EXCELLENCE IS NOT TO BE A QUEST FOR SUPERIORITY

The reason I put that in here is because many in society think that pursuing excellence is parallel with the word excel. The word excel is defined as this: "to do or be better than; surpass; to show superiority, surpass others." The words that are synonymous to excel are: surpass, exceed, transcend, outdo, and outstrip all suggest the concept of going beyond a limit or standard. To excel is to be preeminent (she excels at figure skating) or to be or perform at a level higher than that of another or others (she excelled her father as a lawyer).

So you see, we are not talking about being better than others or being superior to others. That would in no way be Christ-like. Competition or being better than others is a prominent part of the above definitions. But when we think of the pursuit of excellence from a biblical standpoint, is that what we find? No!

As the above terms suggest, those who approach or look at life from the viewpoint of the world typically think competition, or outstripping others, but such is usually done for one's own glory or significance; perhaps even the praise or applause of men. The Author Brian Harbour picks up on this issue in his book *Rising Above the Crowd: Success means being the best.*

> "Excellence means being your best. Success, to many, means being better than everyone else. Excellence means being better tomorrow, than you were yesterday. Success means exceeding the achievements of other people. Excellence means matching your practice with your potential. Excellence isn't determined by comparing our score or performance to someone else's."

The pursuit of excellence comes from doing our best with what we have to God's glory, all the while having a vision to grow and improve. No more keeping score and wondering who is watching from man's standpoint. God is watching. He is enough!

The pursuit of excellence is never a matter of simply choosing between what is good or bad, but choosing what is best or superior. Being wise with your pursuit will better enable you to accomplish what God has designed you to be and do. Do you get it? Are you seeing what excellence is all about? What I understand to be truth is that you can excel, you can be successful, and you can be competitive, without being excellent. That is why we need to strive for excellence in the proper way, the Godly way.

We have to be careful not to get wrapped up in society's way of teaching and showing us what excellence is about. As with most things, society has a warped perspective on what striving for excellence looks like. Christ-like excellence supersedes all others. Ok, let me touch on the statement I made a few sentences back. I wrote that you can excel, you can be successful, and you can be competitive, without being excellent. It's true. Of course, I base this on God's description of excellence. How many "successful" people have you heard about or read about that are crooks, or they treat people badly? That's not excellence. How many people have you heard about or read about that excel at their sport, but have done so because they cheated? That's not excellence either. What about the sports industry in general which is filled with athletes that carry the "I am better than you" attitude? Have you read or heard anywhere about any of them either punching or beating up their wives or girlfriends? How about taking drugs to stay competitive? What about living selfish, greedy lives? These are not traits of excellent individuals. Just because you have money, fame, and notoriety *does not* mean you are excellent.

The pursuit of excellence from a biblical worldview is always connected with the issue of God's values and priorities. This means the pursuit of excellence must include the elimination of some things even though they may be good and legitimate. The principle question is this: based on biblical principles and values are these people/ things in my life God's best or will they hinder God's main objective? If so, they need to be eliminated. We see this truth in Paul's statement in 1 Corinthians 10:23:

"I have the right to do anything," you say—but not everything is beneficial. "I have the right to do anything"—but not everything is constructive. No one should seek their own good, but the good of others." (1 Corinthians 10:23, 24)

Just because they are legitimate does not mean they should be chosen or pursued. Based upon the biblical definition of what excellence is and not society's view or definition, are you striving to be excellent in all that you do?

MY PRAYER:

Heavenly Father, excellence is a word that is often used improperly, so I ask You today to show men what it truly means based on Your definition, to live in excellence. I know that we have merely touched the surface with this chapter, Lord, but I pray that what was passed on will get men to think about and re-evaluate themselves. I pray that men will strive for excellence not only in their jobs or careers, but in their everyday manhood as well. Please draw men unto You so that we will seek You and ask You for wisdom on how to strive for excellence even in our relationships. For the men who have children, may they strive for excellence in being better fathers. God, I know You want men to strive for excellence in everything we do. Your Word says to do it so we may glorify You. I pray men would take more time in striving for excellence in the things that matter and spend less time in the things that don't. Lord, speak to us! Let us know what those things are. Remove those things that waste so much of our time. You are Excellence, and excellence comes from You. May we learn from You so that we can truly glorify and praise Your name. Thank You, Lord!

In Jesus' name, AMEN.

CHAPTER 25

YOU

Y

"So God created mankind (YOU) in his own image, in the image of God he created them (YOU); male and female he created them." (Genesis 1:27)

"Then the Lord God formed a man (YOU) from the dust of the ground and breathed into his nostrils the breath of life, and the man (YOU) became a living being." (Genesis 2:7)

"Without knowing what I am and why I am here, life is impossible". - Leo Tolstoy

"God has given you one face, and you make yourself another."

- William Shakespeare

I really had a tough time hearing from God about a word for "Y". I wasn't sure what God wanted me to write about here. All I kept getting was YOU. I did have a couple of other ideas, but I believe I am supposed to write about YOU. I'm not too sure where I am supposed to go quite yet, but I believe as I continue on, what should be written will come about.

Did you read the two Bible verses? Did you see what I did there? I added the word YOU to make it more personal. That's what this chapter is all about. This chapter is going to allow you to really dig a little deeper inside of yourself. Nothing in this book or any other book is really going to do what God wants unless you really take a look at, you guessed it, YOU!

I know this is a hard task for many men, but it just has to be done. From my experiences with the 12-step program Celebrate Recovery, it can be really difficult for men to open up and examine themselves. This chapter is going to have you realize just how purposeful God created you. You have to know and understand that you are unique in every way. God made you that way. God wants you to see that and so much more.

It's time you find yourself again. Society has a way of slowly chipping away at who God made you to be. If you are not aware of it, you will become a product of that. God wants you to find His purpose for you, not your own purpose. So, the very first step is to know and understand that you are not on earth for your own personal goals and accomplishments. Uh Oh, I done said it, didn't I? Well, it's true. This step was so important yet hard at the same time for me to acknowledge, as it may be for so many of you.

For those of you who have not yet come to terms with this truth, the moment you realize this fact, many things will begin to change in your life.

"Thou art worthy, O Lord, to receive glory and honor and power: for thou hast created all things, and for thy pleasure they are and were created." (Revelation 4:11 KJV)

With this verse you can see that we are created for His purpose, not our own. Why are you the way you are right now? Have you let past situations and circumstances mold you into who you are today? Oh, I forgot to mention. You have to be truthful with yourself or all this is for nothing. Look, there is no guilt here. There is no judgment or shame either. This chapter is going to require you to be a man, be truthful, and be honest. Yes, it can be a hard process, but I promise you as you read and answer the questions, God hears you and He will help you find you, the real you.

The quote at the beginning of the chapter by William Shakespeare really stood out to me.

"God has given you one face, and you make yourself another."

-William Shakespeare

Do you get it? God made you in His image. He made your image exactly how He wanted, but due to situations, circumstances, environment, or other issues you have become this façade of a person. You have let society dictate who you are and what you should be. You have bought into this lie! Don't pretend to think for a minute that you are who you *want* to be. It's not possible because of how we are made. You might think you are who you want to be because you have or are doing some things that make you successful in society. The first time you knew who you were was probably when you were between 10 – 12 years of age. Of course that was not set in stone, because the image you once had has since changed.

I'm merely trying to get you to understand that when you were a child was when you were still the real you. Your wants and dreams were for the most part still pure and innocent. You were still your own person. It wasn't until you reached your early teens that "you" started to disappear into something that had to fit in. Instead of staying true to yourself, you began this long journey of not causing any waves, no confrontations, do as the others do, just fit in. Isn't that what society teaches in order to become successful?

Maybe I am completely off. Perhaps you were the opposite and rebelled against any type of authority. Well, if so, that was just another way of fighting against who you really are.

I know that the story is different for each and every one of us, but it is common to let society or maybe even our families dictate who we are and what we are to be in life.

Influence is a very powerful thing. You don't even realize that you're being influenced until it's happened. That is why wisdom is so important. We need it to discern situations or circumstances before they define us. Too many times in life we are defined by our reactions to something or someone instead of staying true to ourselves in every situation and circumstance.

I want to share with you a little more about my life and how all this applied to me. The only way I was able to accept God's plan for my life was when He began working on my whole person. What I mean by that is He showed me details of when I was a kid, and he reminded me of things throughout my childhood; what I liked as a kid, how I looked as a kid, etc. When I left home at 17, I immediately began looking for my identity, like most of us do. I created this young man from my hurts, my past situations and circumstances. I had lost the kid who liked to get on his bike and ride, or the kid that liked to build models, collect stamps, draw cartoons, and go to school. The kid who once dreamed of becoming a dentist or working for Walt Disney. I reacted to my anger, hurts, situations, and circumstances and became a kid that hurt others.

As I grew up, I became an older version of someone who hurt others. I changed my appearance by lifting weights and taking supplements to grow bigger. I became a bouncer so that I could "legally" fight in clubs. I got a tattoo, wore earrings and evolved into a mean and angry guy all the time. Later in life, I continued with the same patterns. I owned a Harley

Davidson motorcycle and I played the part. Because of the negative things that I experienced in my childhood, I responded or reacted in a way that hurt a number of others. Little did I know, the main one hurting was me. I had lost all sense of who I was, where I was, or where I was going.

"Without knowing what I am and why I am here, life is impossible." - Leo Tolstoy

Life for me was death. I had no life because I had strayed away from the real me. Granted, I didn't know any better. I figured life out along the way. It wouldn't be until maybe less than 10 years ago that God would begin to show me and mold me into a much better version of me. You see, as a child I could have been considered maybe a little "nerdy", because I loved to read and learn. That went away with the ugliness and perversion of what I picked up along the way from society.

One day back in 2010, God reminded me of a photo that my mother took of me when I was a Jehovah's Witness. It was a photo of me in a brown suit and I was on stage giving "my talk", as the Jehovah Witnesses called it. I was maybe 13 and I had prepared my own sermon to give to the congregation. I was in what they called the Theocratic Ministry School, and I was learning to give talks, prepared on my own. I loved it. Some 36 years later or so, He reminds me of this? God impressed upon me to go downstairs and find this photo. I did, and I held it, and I cried. I knew at that moment that life would be even more different than it had been since giving my life over to Him. This was the same time that I got involved with John Maxwell's certification program and Man On Purpose was founded.

Here I am today on chapter 25 of a book that I had no idea that I would be writing. I have by no means arrived, and there is yet much to do, but I know this: allowing God to mold us into who He wants us to be for His purpose is the way to go. What's your story? Remember this chapter is about you. I used my story as an example. I know you have one too. Where is it? I hope you are not keeping it to yourself. Tell it! Tell it now to God. It's not like He doesn't know your story. Write it down. Try to re-track your steps and go back to where the connection was lost. Find out when you lost the real you.

To God, you are very special person. He made you specifically for a purpose. You are not here to just wander around lost and settle for whatever comes your way. God wants you to seize what's yours. You can't get it by going in the opposite direction. I don't care how much money you have, or what position you hold at whatever company. I don't care how many franchises or businesses you own, you will never know life until you've lived the life that God has purposed for you.

If you are reading this and you are doing exactly what you believe God has called you to do, then go out and share with other men. Help them to get to where you are. I say that because I didn't have anyone to help me along the way, but I certainly wish I did. It wouldn't be until 2002 when God introduced me to Carrie, my current wife. She is the one who encouraged me to look within instead of my outside circumstances. Of course, God was overall instrumental in every single aspect, but Carrie has helped me become who I am today.

Here's the thing, unless I faced reality and began to allow my wife and God "in", it would have been all for not. I wouldn't be writing a single word on any page anywhere. I wouldn't have gotten to share Man On Purpose with hundreds of men one on one, or on the radio program. You see, unless you surrender the "society created you", or the "circumstance created you", you will never be able to receive the "God created you".

In order to find out who I was called to be, I had to ask God to reveal it to me. I went through some things that I surely would not have chosen for myself, but often times, in order to find the real you, you have to step outside the current you. You have to be lost, before you can be found. Does that make sense? It is at this point you will discover a lot of untruths about you. This only applies to those who are still struggling with not knowing who they are or where their place is in life. Again, I say, it is definitely not as simple or as easy as I seem to put it. It's a real struggle. My son, Josh, used to say, "The struggle is real." Yes it is. It takes perseverance, diligence, patience, and love, to list a few. If you want to encounter something powerful to get a quicker feel for what life change is all about, sign up for a half marathon. I challenge you.

For me, the whole running phase of my life brought me patience, endurance, perseverance, and victory. All which came from God. I couldn't have done it without Him. As I mentioned earlier in this book, I got into running a few years ago and I don't even know why. It wasn't until later that I received my answer.

I started with a 5k, which is 3.1 miles. I then moved up to a 10k, which is 6.2 miles. Eventually I would then run two 13.2 mile races which are half marathons. The running side of it wasn't too bad, but what stuck out to me the most was that fact that I had a tangible example of endurance, perseverance, patience, and victory. I actually felt what patience feels like. I felt in my body what endurance feels like as well as persevering through the pain and hurts. Finally, crossing the finish line gave me a true feeling of victory! That feeling made it all worthwhile. Competing against someone else was not necessary. If anything, I was competing against myself.

I challenge you. Try it and see if God shows you something. There are all kinds of different ways that God can get something across to you. I worked in the homeless ministry, as I too was homeless for a bit when I left home. Getting involved in this ministry wouldn't have been something I would have chosen, but since I was open and receptive, I did. And looking back, I am so glad that I did because it brought me back to a truthful reality. I was also able to open myself up and begin to love the unlovable. When God allowed for me to participate in Celebrate Recovery on a leadership level, I received much more than I anticipated because I actually went through the program first. I learned so much about myself and how to release how I feel. I literally became more transparent. Again, not something I would have chosen for myself.

I could go on and on with all the things I have been involved with just to find out who I am, and why I am here. What about you? When are you going to stop being prideful and just get involved in something? Not knowing is one thing, but not choosing and not doing is another. I could use a different word here, but I'll hold back using any negative name-calling. Let me just say, it's definitely not the voice of wisdom you are listening to.

Basically, this whole finding your purpose thing is all about surrendering, sacrificing, and separating. You surrender to God and to His will for your life. You sacrifice your wants and desires for those that line up with God's. Lastly, you separate yourself from bad habits, bad environments, and bad individuals. So basically, you're giving up all that is old for all that is new.

"And no one pours new wine into old wineskins. Otherwise, the wine will burst the skins, and both the wine and the wineskins will be ruined. No, they pour new wine into new wineskins." (Mark 2:22)

"Therefore, if anyone is in Christ, the new creation has come: The old has gone, the new is here!" (2 Corinthians 5:17)

This is one of my favorite scriptures. This is you! This can be you if you just let God be God in you; a new creation in Christ, not a creation of society. Let Go and Let God! He wants to show you the real you!

"For you created my inmost being; you knit me together in my mother's womb. I praise you because I am fearfully and wonderfully made; your works are wonderful, I know that full well."
(Psalm 139:13, 14)

Go back and read the entire chapter of Psalm 139. God knows everything about you. He knows what you're going to do or say even before you do it or say it. God only wants the best for you; His best for you. You are fearfully and wonderfully made! Grasp this concept about you and run with it. Remember the words of Leo Tolstoy, "Without knowing what I am and why I am here, life is impossible."

I know, you've read this already. Two other times to be exact, but I had to put it here again. It's so powerful. I went most of my life trying to find the answers to that very statement. Where are you with that? Have you given up and settled in? It doesn't have to be that way, you know. There is so much more to you than the hurting, broken, shameful, lost you. I am grateful to God for helping me find the answers I have been seeking for so long. Now I can truly say, I don't care if I have lots of money or any important title before or after my name. Everything I'm trying to do now is prepare for the next life in heaven with God.

I have yet to receive the exact answer from God as to what I'm going to be doing tomorrow or in the future; but what I have is my identity in

Christ and I know that if I just stay open and receptive, He will guide me. He will open doors that no man can open. I know that an aspect of my purpose is to help people any way I can, and I will try to do that daily. The new me is now making a conscience effort in making someone smile. I'm learning more and more that this life is not about me and what I can get, but it's all about others and what I can give. I leave everything else up to God. He will do whatever He wants with me, and I am okay with it because I trust Him.

I am no longer a Director of Engineering in the hotel business because that's not who I am or what God wants me to do. I will continue to work my current 27.5 hours weekly making $10.00 hour at the fuel station trying to help people with kind words and gestures until God has me do the next thing. I don't know how I'm supposed to get to the next stage of writing this book, but I believe that God does. Oh, if you're reading this right now, then God already provided a way!!

YOU CAN – YOU ARE – YOU WILL

You put those three phrases in your own statements, then lift those statements up to God in prayer. Request that God will guide you towards fulfilling them and watch what happens. If you have received God into your life, you have a great helper living inside you – The Holy Spirit. Now put Him to work!

MY PRAYER: Heavenly Father, Your Word says that we are

fearfully and wonderfully made. It says that You knew us and knit us together in our mother's womb. Help us to understand these truths. Help us find out who we are in You, not what society is telling us we ought to be. You, Lord, are our Creator and only You can help us find who we are supposed to be. No matter what we are doing right now, we want to hand it all over to You. Please sort through, take away, and rearrange our lives so that it comes into alignment with who we need to be for You. I thank You for giving us life. We want to be better stewards over this new life that You have given us. I truly desire a greater understanding on why we are here. We are here for You, Lord. You have us where we are today for Your reasoning at this moment in history. We surrender to You today. We want what You want for us; the best!

Thank You, Lord!
In Jesus' name, AMEN!

CHAPTER 26

ZEAL

"Never be lacking in zeal, but keep your spiritual fervor, serving the Lord." (Romans 12:11)

I have to admit; I don't think I've ever used this word. I mean I have read about zeal in the Bible, but actually using it myself, I don't believe I have, like ever. My wife Carrie thought it was a good word to write about. I initially didn't want to, but I also didn't hear too many choices coming from God. How many words can one write about that is Biblical and begins with the letter Z? This just might be the only one. In doing some extracurricular reading on this word, I came across some explanations that used zeal in the same context as passion. I believe the two are intertwined, but not necessarily the same. Before we go any further let's see if I can clarify using what I found in Wiktionary.

Zeal: the fervor or tireless devotion for a person, cause, or ideal and determination in its furtherance; diligent enthusiasm; powerful interest.

Passion:

1) any great, strong, powerful emotion, especially romantic love or hate.

2) Pursuing something with excitement, passion, affection, or enthusiasm, with the goal to accomplish, encounter, or obtain it.

I believe, the main difference is that passion is the "feeling" and zeal is the "doing". When you are zealous you have great determination to accomplish something; the "doing". Zeal requires action. You can't be zealous while sitting on the couch. Think about it...The man was zealous in his pursuit while sitting in his comfy chair? I don't think so! So, what is Paul telling us in the chapter verse?

"Never be lacking in zeal, but keep your spiritual fervor, serving the Lord."

How about this: Never be lacking in tireless devotion, but keep your strong feeling of excitement and enthusiasm, serving the Lord. You see what I did there? The "strong feeling of excitement and enthusiasm" could actually be "passion"? Think about what you currently are giving "tireless devotion" to.

What are you passionate about? I know for a lot of men it's usually their jobs or careers. As you can see here, it's to God only that we should not just be devoted to, but it should be a "tireless devotion". You can be excellent at your jobs or careers without having to devote everything to them. There are people who are "devoted" to their country and not to God. I really don't understand that since God created this country. I mean I served in the Army and I get the concept of devoting myself to country, but I have since learned God is the one I should be devoted to.

Devoting or zealously seeking after anything else other than God leaves us empty and unfulfilled. We were created to be devoted individuals, that's why people have this need to devote themselves to something. That's not how God wanted it though. *Something* however isn't good enough. We are supposed to be devoted to God and to Him only. I guess it's easier to devote, or fervently go after something or someone that you can see and continually lets you down. There is absolutely no long-term satisfaction in going after everything in this world. Humanity invests so much time and money in things that bring no lasting value. That's why we have God's promises and assurances in the Bible.

"But seek first the kingdom of God and his righteousness, and all these things will be added to you." (Matthew 6:33)

"And let us not grow weary of doing good, for in due season we will reap, if we do not give up." (Galatians 6:9)

"And whatever you do, in word or deed, do everything in the name of the Lord Jesus, giving thanks to God the Father through him." (Colossians 3:17)

The verses could go on and on, but then I would end up with a big chunk of the Bible in this chapter! If you read your Bible on a regular basis, then you know what I'm saying. For those of you who do not read your Bible, all I can say is you're missing out. Oh, and READ YOUR BIBLE!

I was sitting here listening to worship music and the song, **"Set A Fire"** by Will Reagan & United Pursuit came on. It reminded me about the difference between passion and zeal. There's a line in the song that says,

> *Set a fire down in my soul*
> *That I can't contain,*
> *That I can't control,*
> *I want more of you, God*

Is this passion or is this zeal? Going after God like an out of control fire? I believe the pursuit of going after God is definitely demonstrating what zeal is; but what about the "fire down in my soul"? Isn't that more along the lines of a burning, passionate desire of wanting or yearning for God? I'll leave that one up to your own discretion.

I believe it's definitely a mix of the two. Another question that came up is which comes first, zeal or passion? Can one be zealous and not passionate about something; even pursuing after God? Does it even matter which comes first? These are just questions or thoughts that I challenge you to ask yourself. There isn't really a right or wrong answer to these questions.

If you were wondering what I would answer to the above questions, then my answer would be that God wants us to have both towards Him. If you are passionate about God and His will for your life, then I believe you will be zealous in pursuing and serving Him. I came across a sermon preached by a guy named J.C. Ryle given in the late 1800's entitled "Christian Zeal". I can only put a couple of paragraphs in here, but it is definitely worth reading the whole thing. It actually can be purchased as a live sermon. He writes:

My object in this message is to plead the cause of zeal in religion. I believe we ought not to be afraid of it, but rather to love and admire it. I believe it to be a mighty blessing to the world and the origin of countless benefits to mankind. I want to remind Christians that "Zealot" was a name given to one of the Apostles of our Lord Jesus Christ, and to persuade them to be zealous men and women. I ask every one of you to give me your attention while I tell you something about zeal. Listen to me for your own sake, for the sake of the world, for the sake of the Church of our Christ. Listen to me and by God's help I will show you that to be "zealous" is to be wise. Zeal in Christianity is a burning desire to please God, to do His will, and to advance His glory in the world in every possible way. It is a desire, which is not natural to men or women. It is a desire which the Spirit puts in the heart of every believer when they are converted to Christ, however, a desire which some believers feel so much more strongly than others that they alone deserve to be called "zealous" men and women. This desire is so strong, when it really reigns in a person, that it impels them to make any sacrifice, to go through any trouble, to deny themselves anything, to suffer, to work, to labor, to toil, to spend themselves and be spent, and even to die, if only they can please God and honor Christ. A zealous person in Christianity is preeminently a person of one thing. It is not enough to say that they are earnest, strong, uncompromising, meticulous, wholehearted, and fervent in spirit. They only see one thing, they care for one thing, they live for one thing, they are swallowed up in one thing; and that one thing is to please God.

Reading some of his sermon made me think about how watered down our zealous pursuit for God is in today's society. I'm not saying that applies to every single Christian alive, I mean I can't know that. I do however believe that generally speaking, if every Christian were as zealous as this author writes about, then Christ followers would be known all over the world? The depth of this type of zealousness is incomprehensible to so many individuals; including me.

The more I read commentaries, discussions, or sermons from that time period, I see just how far away I really am from getting it right. I think that men today need so much more grace and mercy than those from earlier centuries. We read examples of zealous people in the Bible like Elijah and think, *how on earth can I ever measure up to such a man?*

I don't know what the answer is, truth be told.

Nevertheless, I do know that you and I can only do and be what God needs us to be in today's society. I'm not sure if comparing back then to right now is even the right thing to do. All I know is this: I sincerely want to continue my pursuit after God, fervently, zealously, and with much passion. I have tried to be obedient and do what God wants me to do. I have told you stories about businesses and careers that God obviously closed the doors to just so I could serve Him.

In my pursuit after God, He has led me right here, writing these words on these pages of this book. I have learned by being zealous after Him, He opens doors and provides opportunities that I would have never thought about walking through.

"It is fine to be zealous, provided the purpose is good, and to be so always, not just when I am with you." (Galatians 4:18)

I believe one of the biggest challenges to overcome in today's society is avoiding all the distractions. Unfortunately we give into those distractions instead of paying attention to God. Everything else looks good, tastes good, feels good, sounds good, and smells good. In case you didn't notice, I just covered the five senses. That is what appeals to us more than staying zealous in our godly pursuit and staying focused on His plans for us.

Society has perfected, with the help of Satan, our adversary, a way of pulling us away from what is truly important. Satan even uses certain individuals to misinterpret the Scriptures and preach the "prosperity gospel," as if it was something that God had in mind for each and every one of us.

If you take a deeper look throughout the Bible, you will see that the more one goes after riches and wealth, the less zealous he is for God. It becomes being zealous for self. We are definitely good at that. We are zealous in so many other areas, but when you are told that type of zealousness is not biblical, you want to get mad or even deny God. Our heavenly Father wants us to fully understand that everything He wants for us is always His best.

Being zealous after God is a practice that we all could get better at. It will not improve our own selfish worship, but our worship to God. After all, if you say that you love God and strive to be Christ-like, then why wouldn't you want to be more zealous in your pursuit of your Creator?

After all the reading, research, and writing of this chapter, I have come to realize that my zealous pursuit of God is pretty weak. I want to give Him more and more of myself. I want everyone that comes in contact with me to know that I am a zealous Christ follower. On my last day alive, I would love to hear these words from those that know me: "In every way, and in every area of his life, Richard was very zealous after God."

What about you? Would those who know you be able to say that? Ask yourself, what are you zealous after? Is it God or is it other things? When I meet Jesus, face to face, I want him to say, **"Well done, good and faithful servant."** Not… **"So, because you are lukewarm—neither hot nor cold—I am about to spit you out of my mouth."**

What about you?

MY PRAYER:
Heavenly Father, What an amazing topic to write about. Thank you for these words. If we as Christian men are supposed to be as zealous as what I wrote about, then I believe we need to be praying a whole bunch! Lord, we need you to help us, and show us how to be more zealous after you. I believe we men know how to be zealous after a lot of other things that are only hindrances to going after you the way we should. I pray that what has been written in this final chapter stirs up a motion for men to seek after what's most important, and that's you God. I lift this excerpt from the sermon that J.C Ryle wrote up to you Lord, because it's how I believe we need to be if we want to truly please you.

A zealous person in Christianity is preeminently a person of one thing. It is not enough to say that they are earnest, strong, uncompromising, meticulous, wholehearted, and fervent in spirit. They only see one thing, they care for one thing, they live for one thing, they are swallowed up in one thing; and that one thing is to please God.

Lord, may we all learn to strive for this level of zealousness after you!

In Jesus' name, AMEN!

AUTHOR'S TESTIMONY

My story begins in Parkersburg, West Virginia on July 10, 1966. My mother and father were not married. She was a bartender/waitress and he was a musician. He played in a band by night and worked in a Borg Warner plant by day. I have two younger brothers from my mother, one of which is a half-brother due to my mom cheating on my dad. He grew up with us, my dad accepted him as his own. I had no clue about this until I was 15 years old or so.

My brothers and I spent a lot of time with babysitters as our parents both worked nightshifts. One afternoon my mother decided she had enough of the abuse my dad was giving her and she left to Florida with us. I was 7 at this time. We lived in different hotels and we were left alone every night. My mother used to send a taxi driver to our room with dinner. One night I woke up to a room full of noises and naked people. Of course, I didn't know what it was at that time.

Shortly after, my mother dropped me and my brothers off to a foster home. That would be the last time I would ever see her. I am still unclear as to how long we were there, but my dad found us and we were reunited with him and his German girlfriend; who would later become our new mom. She had a daughter that was the same age as my middle brother.

My dad met her at the club he played at and she was a bartender there, go figure. She was already moved in by the time we came back from Florida.

At this time, I guess I was 8 years old and in the 2nd grade. I don't know when the physical abuse started exactly, but it wasn't too long after we returned. At the age of 10 or 11, I was forced to do sexual things to our babysitter. At the age of 11 or 12, I was forced to do sexual things, not only to the babysitter, but also to my uncle. He made me do things to his two friends that lived down the street from our house as well. Sadly, this happened a few times while he was there with us. Of course, he used the fear I had of my dad to coerce me. So, from a young age I was already introduced to verbal, physical, and sexual abuse. The physical abuse lasted the longest. I endured severe physical violence all the way up to the age of 16 from my dad.

In 1978, at the age of 12, our German mom introduced us to the Jehovah's Witnesses. We began going to the Kingdom Hall regularly. My dad gave up drinking, drugs and gambling. I thought we were going to be a normal family. Yeah not so much. The physical violence continued. At this point my mom was even participating in the abuse towards us. We also were humiliated and had to endure verbal abuse from her as well.

In 1980, my mom finally talked my dad into moving to Germany. We couldn't believe we were moving to Germany! We sold everything and moved. We stayed with my mom's parents for a while. We continued to go to the Kingdom Hall as her parents were devout Jehovah's Witnesses. As long as we were living with the grandparents, the abuse was very minimal.

My family moved and finally we got our own apartment. My dad was playing in a band again as well as working during the week. The drinking and smoking started back up and so did the physical and verbal abuse. It was all pretty bad.

In 1983, after finishing school and in the midst of trade school, I was barely 17 and I had enough. The physical abuse was just horrendous at this point. I told myself that I had to leave. Either I would end up killing my dad or he would end up killing me. I left and I was homeless. I lived in storage rooms and depending on where I ended up each day, I slept in abandoned cars that were in a parking garage. I found places to clean up and I began stealing clothes and food for survival.

I hung out every night in the club and no one ever knew my situation. For a while, I stayed in my friend's dad's storage shed in their back yard until a female offered me a place to stay. She was older than me and of course she expected something... I lost my virginity and so began my sexual rampage. From 1984 - 1988 I will sum up those years with the following words: relationships, sex, drugs, alcohol, rage, severe violence, money, stealing, fighting, disregard for any authority, abuse, on and on and on.

I was living a complete reckless and out of control life. I even joined a gang. I did whatever I wanted, whenever I wanted, and however I wanted. I had to leave Germany. My friend, whose step-dad was retiring out of the Army back in America, wanted to go. He asked me if I wanted to come with him and I said yes.

So, I left Germany and there I was in the USA by 1988. *Things are definitely going to be better now,* I said to myself. I lived in Lawrenceville with my friend and his parents, worked at Winn Dixie up the street and at Mervyn's at Gwinnett Place Mall. It didn't take too long until I found a girlfriend, she started at Mervyn's the same day I did. Before our training had ended we were a couple.

By December 31, 1989 we were married. I had already signed to go into the Army and got called in February 1990. I was stationed in Panama which was perfect for her being that she was Dominican. Shortly after arriving there, we had massive problems. She wanted to leave and go back to the U.S.

Our first son was born September 18, 1991, there in the military hospital in Panama. My wife had returned shortly before his birth and she brought her mother. Everything seemed to be okay considering. I guess the first of my marital affairs started sometime in 92' after she had left again to go back to the U.S. From 1992 – 2002, I was married but I had no marriage. I got out of the Army in 1994. By 1996 we had our second son, but by then, and actually during his birth, I had already been involved in so many extra marital affairs it wasn't funny. These years consisted of out of control, intimate relationships.

I worked as a bouncer for most of the years after the military, so I had access to all the women I wanted. These years consisted of unexplainable sex. For the first time in many years, I was involved with not only many women, but several men. I was very violent, with an explosive temper. I was into body building and taking steroid-like drugs. I was 250 lbs. at that time and I was extremely verbally abusive to my wife and kids.

I did what I wanted, when I wanted, and how I wanted. Needless to say, it all came to an end in 2002 when I was arrested for losing my temper one night while I was trying to get ready for work. I was bonded out by a woman that I was having an affair with. She had just delivered my youngest son in March. My Dominican wife found out about her, but she didn't know about the baby. I had left my cell on the table while the other woman was calling trying to see where I was. She worked at the club where I bounced. When I came back to the apartment three days later, I was shocked to find all my stuff in boxes outside of the apartment.

I had no car, and no place to go. I stayed with my friend for a few weeks and also got a car from his past roommate. All of this led up to me having to take a position that required me to live on the property. The person who hired me is actually my wife today. The next few years were a mess.

By July 2002, I was hired by Carrie and moved into The White Columns Inn. I was hired to clean up the property as a Courtesy Officer. I had my child's mother living with me on the property as well. I finally gave up bouncing and stayed working on the property, but I had several other relationships going on. I broke them off and the relationship with my son's mother just so that I could pursue other relationships. I became involved with Carrie at this point as well as several other women and men. I was out of control! Sexual gratification was the only thing on my mind.

With Carrie it was different; she shared Bible verses with me and she helped me to start seeing some things about myself. The things she shared, no one else had ever told me before. Needless to say, Carrie and I stuck together even though she had 4 kids of her own. For the next few years, up to 2005, we moved several times and all the while we stayed together. Despite my verbally and physically abusive to her and the kids, we stayed together.

One night during a fight in September 2005, still living an ongoing lifestyle of out of control sex, affairs, violence, and abuse, I exclaimed with a few choice words that we were going to church. The next morning, we walked into Victory World Church in Norcross, Georgia. After one month of attending that church, I surrendered my life to God. After this point, things would never be the same.

In 2006, I was water baptized. Shortly after that I received the baptism of the Holy Spirit. On August 18, 2006 the divorce that my Dominican wife filed was now complete. On August 24, 2006 at around 2:00 pm I heard God tell me, "It was time." Shortly after that day, Carrie and I were married.

In 2007 Carrie and I became involved in the homeless ministry at our church. In the same year, I became part of the Security Ministry. In 2009, Carrie and I were chosen to help start Celebrate Recovery in our church.

I was the men's co-leader of the Ministry. As I facilitated the groups, I had to go through the 12-step program myself. Others and I really started to see a big change. I was able to deal with "stuff" that I thought I was healed from. I began to truly receive healing.

December 17, 2010, I lost yet another job. I had been in the hotel industry since 2002 and I worked my way up to multi-property Director of Engineer in one of the leading hotel corporations. I hadn't a clue what God was about to do in my life. But in August 2011, I was blessed with the opportunity to be trained and certified by the one and only, John Maxwell. By February 18, 2012 I received my certificate as a Certified Teacher, Coach, and Speaker with the John Maxwell Company in Palm Beach Gardens, Florida at a 3 day conference. When I came back, I continue with MasterMind groups, teaching the John Maxwell topics. I facilitated a group in "Everyone Communicates, Few Connect". Prior to this I facilitated "The 21 Irrefutable Laws of Leadership". I soon came to find that God had a different plan for me.

On Saturday April 18, 2012 at about 9:00 a.m., I woke up to what I felt God speaking to me. I got up and grabbed my iPad and began writing down what I was hearing. I know He told me to start Man on Purpose and it was to be about empowering men to become the men they are intended to be with purpose, on purpose. I was also told to put together a men's event.

Yikes, I thought.

On August 04, 2012 I held my first men's event at World Outreach Church for all Nations in Lawrenceville. I taught John Maxwell's book *The 15 Laws of Personal Growth*. On my birthday July 10, 2012 I was able to promote this event with an interview on the JOY FM 93.3 radio station. On August 1, 2012, I was on Atlanta Live to promote the event, which is WATC Channel 57, a local Atlanta television channel.

On September 21, 2012, I did another radio interview on The JOY FM 93.3 with Michael Southwell to promote the very first, God Belongs In My City prayer walk. This took place on Saturday September 29, 2012 at Centennial Olympic Park. Along with Mary Held, I was able to speak about www.godsvote.com. We had a booth set up with banner for promotion of this message. It was a fun day.

On September 26, 2012 I was interviewed again on Atlanta Live to talk about www.godsvote.com. This time, it was a collaborative effort with Mary and I. We pushed her vision for MaryLovesLife and the fact that God belongs in our votes.

On September 27, 2012, my first BlogTalkRadio show aired. Man On Purpose is the name of it. One particular show I had Michael Southwell, aka Pastor Mike, on to share more about the prayer walk, God Belongs In My City. Now here I am in 2015 writing my first book, *The ABC's of Man On Purpose* by faith.

I share my story with you for one reason. I want you to see once I allowed God to enter my life how things began to transform. He is the one I give credit to for allowing me to become the man I was intended to be with purpose, on purpose... My thoughts, desires, actions and life are in line with His plans and purposes now only because I am surrendered to Him. I have to die to my selfish desires daily and allow the Holy Spirit to guide me. I truly believe we must seek Him first for wisdom. It's not about preference; it's not about common sense. It's all about obedience. With God all things are possible!

"Submit yourselves, then, to God. Resist the devil, and he will flee from you." (James 4:7 NIV)

"Therefore, if anyone is in Christ, the new creation has come; the old has gone, the new is here!" (2 Corinthians 5:17 NIV)

"The life I once knew is forever gone. I am still of course, and will always be, as long as I am here on earth, a "work in progress".

– Richard Rice

http://manonpurpose.org

UPDATE

Hey Guys,

I just wanted to give you the lastest goings on. As of October 22, 2015 Carrie and I have relocated to Irving, Texas. Carrie received an amazing job offer, so after much prayer we went ahead and moved. Carrie is from Texas anyway, and she has been wanting to go back for a long time now. I believe God has allowed this move for something pretty awesome. We are currently attending Robert Morris' church, GATEWAY CHURCH in Southlake, Texas. I am currently seeking yet again, another part time hourly position so that I can focus on promoting this book through whatever means God sees appropriate. I would kindly ask you to lift MAN ON PURPOSE ministry and me up in prayer. I believe that God will open doors for me to promote this book at men's events, conferences, and book signing/launch events. Thank you guys very much for your support! Oh, Hey I would love to hear from you; your thoughts or comments. Contact me via email: admin@manonpurpose.org

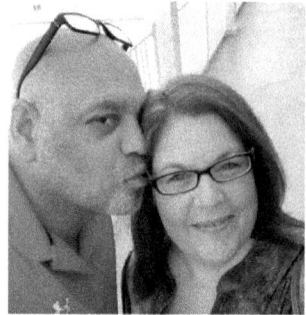

Blessings,

Richard Rice

4 As a prisoner for the Lord, then, **I urge you to live a life worthy of the calling you have received.** [2] **Be completely humble and gentle; be patient, bearing with one another in love.** [3] Make every effort to keep the unity of the Spirit through the bond of peace. [4] There is one body and one Spirit, just as you were called to one hope when you were called; [5] one Lord, one faith, one baptism; [6] one God and Father of all, who is over all and through all and in all.

Ephesians 4: 1-6

www.ingramcontent.com/pod-product-compliance
Lightning Source LLC
Chambersburg PA
CBHW051816090426

42736CB00011B/1500